Spiritual Answers

for Working as a Healing Channel

WENDY EDWARDS

BALBOA.
PRESS

A DIVISION OF HAY HOUSE

Balboa Press books may be ordered through booksellers or by contacting:

Balboa Press
A Division of Hay House
1663 Liberty Drive
Bloomington, IN 47403
www.balboapress.com.au
1-(877) 407-4847

ISBN: 978-1-4525-0386-8 (sc)
ISBN: 978-1-4525-0387-5 (e)

Printed in the United States of America

Balboa Press rev. date: 02/27/2012

Dedication

Thanks to my family and friends for helping me produce this book and to the spiritual world for working in the Oneness with me, so that I could share this information with others.

—Wendy Edwards

Acknowledgements

To Ray and my sons for their love, patience and support over the years.

Special thanks to Ray and Joy for their editing contributions.

To Susanne for her love, guidance and timely generosity.

Thanks to Anna for doing the photograph for my books.

Special mention to Paula, Mavreen and Drew for their spiritual messages of hope and their loving support.

Thanks also to Julie, Joy, Angela, Rachela, Kirsty, Mel, Malgosia, and Virginia for their help, encouragement and friendship during the writing of these books.

You are the Oneness, so in this awareness let the light flow through you.

Contents

Introduction

The wisdom of the Light

This book explains the intricacies of the different energies and the realities of working with the Light. I begin with a section on working as a healing channel, followed by ways to keep your aura and personal space safe and protected. Added to this, the workings of the aura and the use of the many lights is discussed. Anyone actively working in this area or about to embark on their own spiritual journey can benefit from this information.

This is the third book of the series. "Spiritual Answers to Guide Your Life" and "Spiritual Answers for Health and Happiness" precede it.

It took me hundreds of hours of working with the Light to come to an understanding of the way energy works. Even then, as I progressed, I felt there was more and more to learn. In the following pages, I have included all I have come to understand. You must decide what is applicable to your life and work. We all come from different worlds and backgrounds, so it is important that you take from the book what applies to your reality.

If you are already working as a light worker, your experiences will be different to mine and as such, my writing may concur with yours or not. Therefore, use your own instincts as a guide.

I hope you are enjoying learning about the spiritual work as much as I am, and I wish you well on your life's journey.

Working as a Healing Channel

Never compare yourself to others. Be happy for their happiness.
Be joyful for their gifts. But also know you are exactly where you
have chosen to be, and your path too can be lined with gold.

Healing and curing

As a healing channel, you are basically a channel for the light. All healing comes from the universal light. While we all can carry the same light, some channels are clearer and more powerful than others and so the outcome is better.

Even so, the healing is always dependent on the receiver. You could be Jesus or Buddha channeling great healing light but if the person wants to stay sick, they will. Free will decides how much change occurs. Always remember, we are not the healer. We are only the channel. It will keep you grounded and less involved with ego. I struggled with some poor responses to the healing work until I began to understand my part. We are only responsible for the energy exchange. The person holds all the answers, and it is always their choice. Never take responsibility for the outcome. Remember, we live in the world of free will.

Of course, positive healings are uplifting. After all that time and effort it seems to make the whole thing worthwhile. Mission accomplished. However, people are curious beings. Many people may choose to revert to their previous aural pattern soon after the healing. I noticed that when some clients left my place, all their chakras were spinning correctly, yet by the time they reached home, they had reset their aura. If I had asked them whether they had received the healing, the answer would have been yes, but I knew otherwise. I think some people needed the old pattern to be able to function in their current world.

Curing is more complicated than healing because it has to operate on a very deep level. We can cure ourselves if given the skills and right intention. Curing means digging deep and facing the real issues underpinning the illness. It means having to "feel" your way out and this can be very painful emotionally. So, most people stick to healing the symptoms without addressing the underlying cause. A skilled healer can assist in curing us when we are aligned with the same purpose. Still, while he or she can help with the energetic shifts, we will have to be willing to make the necessary changes in our life.

Some changes may be to do with our diet and exercise habits because on a physical level the body will need to be clearing too. Nutritious foods and cleansing herbs will assist us.

Emotional blocks will have to be faced and worked through. Often, the problem originates from these very blocks. We might have to release them and feel the fear, anger and hurt. In the process, there can be anxious and angry days while the emotions surface. It would be good not to feel all those awful pains, but without expression, they can't always be cleared from our aura.

On some levels, we may not want to let them go, for after decades of carrying them, we can feel naked and vulnerable without them. Anger can make us feel strong, fear can keep us in a safe place as it blocks progress, and hurt can keep us attached to the persons responsible. To let go is challenging.

Mentally, we may hold thought patterns that have made us ill. Honestly, altering the way we think is very difficult. Deep-rooted habits take time to change. Maybe we have been thinking in these ways for years, maybe even lifetimes. At times, we can have trouble recognizing negative thoughts. They have protected us and been part of our lives for so long that we no longer see them.

Added to this is the spiritual component to curing. Typically, the illness is firmly rooted in some spiritual lesson. It may be forgiveness, acceptance or balancing karma. An insight for us will be our initial resistance to change. We may not want to forgive someone who has wronged us. We may not want to face a poor marriage and leave. We may not want to tackle our inner soul's yearning. Lack of creative expression is frequently involved in serious illness, the slow death of an unfulfilled soul. Our soul needs expression to be healthy, and so any block around this expression can hinder our progress. If you are creative, your soul will need expression to keep you well.

Tackling all these levels is our only hope of cure. No one can do it for us. For it comes from deep within. The cure lies in the soul. Sickness is an opportunity for growth and understanding. On occasions, its terminal quality becomes a vehicle for the journey to the next dimension.

Not curing it is not a failure. It is merely a lesson for the soul. Never criticize others or yourself for not being cured. Perhaps the soul's intention had nothing to do with curing, but all hinged on learning.

Our spiritual intentions

Once we embark upon this work as a channel our intention becomes extremely significant, because it can advance our healing and channeling capacity. Our intention is the basic belief system we use when working. With trust and faith, much more can be sourced through us. With these two elements, Spirit can move heaven and earth, for we are not bound on the earth plane. Trust and faith mean we are part of the process, but not in charge. We trust whatever our guardians say or do, for trust allows the light to flow through our aura evenly and at a higher rate. Of course, we are the messengers, and as such, there are areas that we become responsible for. However, for the most part, Spirit is in command.

Keep in mind that doubt blocks energetic flow and can bring our vibrational rate down. It is human to doubt, but when working in this realm it has no place. Once doubt seeps in, it can alter the outcome. When we work with Spirit, our intention needs to be as clear as possible. I ask for the right light, guidance and healing for the person who I am working with. By giving over to a greater power, I know the work will be perfect for this time and space.

We are never the healer or reader. We are always the instrument. As such, let Spirit choose the song to play through us.

If ego gets in the way, we will be trying to run the show. Whenever we work with Spirit in this manner, all kinds of things can go wrong. Ego will keep us in the lower vibrations and being unable to channel a high vibration, the work coming through will be compromised.

I always aim for the highest guidance and healing. Why work in lower dimensions? Aim for the greatest vibration your aura can access. Ask for the best healers to work with you. In my healings, I ask for particular doctors to attend and assist in the healings. We can ask for emotional healers who will channel wise and comforting words. Herbalists can be called in to give advice on beneficial plant medicines the person can use. There have been some sessions in which people felt chiropractic work being done on them.

When there is a tough case to work on, ask for extra help and guidance. Remember, that if needed, spiritual surgery can be done. I feel we have to be quite skilled to work with Spirit in these situations. It usually involves a good working relationship with our guides. Healers capable of doing this type of surgery have to be in tune and very obedient. Some healers are doing these precise surgeries without realizing it because their guardians have already established a clear and workable arrangement. I was told I had previously performed these procedures before the human part of me was aware of it.

Work with the intention to raise your vibration and, in doing so, you will ascend. Intend to be a clear and open channel, a pure interface between our dimension and Spirit, and to work in a realm full of love and light.

Channeling the light energy

Some light workers can make the mistake of channeling their own energy, instead of using the incoming energy. We all have energy flowing in and out of our own aura, which can be used to aid others. We can send our own energy to another person, or we can give it away. However, although we can work in this manner, it is not a good habit to channel in this fashion. It is like a blood transfusion. We can make more blood, but if we keep allowing the blood to flow out, our own body will eventually deteriorate, and we won't be able to make up the loss. A similar thing happens with energy.

Energy depletion comes on slowly, but eventually will manifest in the physical world. Healers and light workers regularly suffer from burnout. From the start, when you work, intend on manifesting and channeling external energy through you to others. In this way, you retain an intact aura, and in the long run, your health will not be compromised. Burnout can happen when we cease to listen to our own energy levels. Channeling energy requires lifting our vibration and maintaining it while working. It can put a strain on our aura, so be aware of this phenomenon.

Another reason to use external energy is due to its vibrational quality. If we channel the energy, the optimum vibrational rate will be sourced from Spirit. Remember that your personal energy rate might not suit the receiver, and if your vibration is running too fast or too slow for the recipient, the best outcome will not be reached. I trust Spirit will deliver the right light for the occasion. Healers and readers are people too. They all have their own blocks and issues to deal with, so their energies will never be as pure as the light flowing from Spirit.

For example, say you need to refill someone's base chakra, but your own base is already depleted. When you tap into your own aura not much will be available, and so the person who is receiving the light won't get enough. In addition, by using your own aural energy, you will have less. However, if you channel energy from the spiritual world, there is a limitless amount day or night. The light is cleaner and vibrates into the aura at exactly the right rate for the person.

I never believe my energy is better than what is possible from Spirit. I bow to them. For all of my work, I choose to use light from the higher beings.

How to work with your guides

When I began to do healing work, I had no idea what I was doing. Initially, I stood near the person and held my hands above their stomach as they lay on the massage table. I was so naïve and had nobody to ask. My first few attempts were memorable, to say the least, as I tried my new skills on my poor husband. During my initial, tentative healings, I was guided to step out of the way. To do this, I had to visualize standing out of my physical body and standing beside myself. This action then allowed my guardian to step into my aura and commence the work. When you try to step out and relinquish all control, it can be quite challenging.

The reason I was told to stand out was due to my inability to let go of all control and allow the guide to take over totally. It can take courage handing over to Spirit when we first begin our journey. It was quite hard to keep myself out of the way, so to speak.

At the beginning, the energy of our aura and the new guide needs to blend together. We need to become used to one another. I suggest you use this method until you don't need to. It may take a few healings or many months working in this fashion until you can discard the process. I found that in time it became unnecessary. As with most things the more we do them, the better we become.

When I began, I would step aside, do the work with my guide and afterwards step back into my physical body. Nowadays, we work easily together. Our vibrations blend. The reason that Spirit also uses this process is to get us slowly used to the change of vibration in our aura. Channeling and healing work uses our body. A higher vibrational being working with us does initially put a strain on our aura. For many of us, it is a "new" experience here in this life. Therefore, we need to adjust slowly to the situation.

Once you are working, if you feel you need to move your hands or walk around the person and focus somewhere else, do so. You will be guided. I remember when my hands started moving, and I didn't know what to do. My husband suggested that I follow them, which I did. As I walked around the table following my hands, we both began to laugh. It was so obvious, yet I had missed their cue. I suspect my guides were laughing too and shaking their heads in disbelief.

It is a wonderful and exciting experience to begin our healing work. I believe if we keep in mind that all of us exist in a dense space and take the time to synergize with our healing guides, then our connection can only be strengthened. Healing work requires patience and dedication, but the rewards for you and others are immeasurable. Enjoy!

Different sensations in healing work

Once you begin doing light work, you will encounter many unusual sensations coming from the aura. Some will be subtle, while others will be very noticeable. Not only will pain be sensed, but there may also be feelings that you have not yet encountered. There are numerous sensations. The Chinese have a name for some of these energies. In a sense, we are like acupuncturists, except that we are working on larger channels, and so when we do healing work, we can feel similar energies. I have felt the energies identified by acupuncturists. They are damp, dry, heat, wind and cold.

I can regularly feel the heat. There can also be damp heat, which I know by its sauna quality. Ordinary heat does not feel wet. As we work on the person, the energies can change. It can begin with a hot quality, and then develop into damp heat. Although the energies are both heat, the effects on the aura are quite different.

Cold is easily felt. If there is a great deal of cold or if layers of cold come off from the aura, your hands can become very cold as well. Quite often the person you are working on may complain of feeling cold. Cold wind, like the heat situation can frequently be sensed. Wind sometimes comes off the body. It will feel like a breeze under or around your hands. When it first happened, I checked the window to see where the wind was coming from. Noticing that the window was closed, I mentioned it to my client. He admitted he could actually feel the wind pouring out of his heart chakra. We both had a chuckle about his "wind."

In Chinese energy work, there is another energy called dry. I must admit to never quite working out how dry feels. Maybe I will in the future.

There are many other sensations and pains unique to the aura. Tingling is very common and denotes a release of energy. Prickly "pins and needles" is mostly felt when fear is being released from the aura. Sometimes, you can feel bubbles collecting under your hands. The energy bubbles rise up off the aura and bounce under your palms. Frequently, my hands have gone numb, and at times, it has been coupled with the "pins and needles" sensation. Your client might even tell you that they can't feel their legs or arms.

And then there is the pain. Some pains are terrible, and you have to keep working until they pass. In some healings, I have prayed for it to end. It never ceases to amaze me how much awful pain one aura can hold. When the pain energy is being shifted out of the energy body, the person might experience pain too. Encourage them to let it go and view it as a sign of release.

Another strange thing can occur. When you are working your feet can become very sore. When we are channeling our soles can be sucked tightly to the floor, and it can really hurt. I have learnt to accept it is part of the healing and to wait for it to pass. Try not to break the earth energy connection by moving your feet.

When doing the healing work your arms can be held out in certain positions for long periods of time. In our world, people have used this practice as a torture technique. However, in healing work it is called channeling. I am used to it now. I accept that if it lasts for a long time my hands and arms may ache and go stiff. It is all part of the work and not detrimental to you long-term.

Sighing from the person and emotional outbursts like crying are positive signs of release. Other physical signs can be when the body twitches and the digestion gurgles.

Healing work is a gift and a joy. Nonetheless, it can be uncomfortable and painful. If you can handle that, then I believe it is the most wonderful gift we can possess. To be able to take another's pain away is a wondrous act of love.

Transferring emotions

There can be an emotional transfer of energy during healings and readings. Unwittingly, our emotions can influence the work. If we are dealing with particular emotions, these energies can be transferred easily into the other person's aura. Usually, this transfer is unintentional, and occurs on a subliminal level.

For example, the person we are working on may be more emotionally up than we are on the day. Now, the higher energy always takes on the lower one. So in this situation the client is in better shape than the healer. After the session, the healer's emotional energy might have affected the client without anyone even realizing it. People who work with energy need to consider this aspect because there are many healing situations in which this transfer occurs. Naturally, it is always better for the recipient to be worked on by a balanced, high vibrating person; otherwise their energy could be used to fill us up.

I have experienced being worked on by an unbalanced person. When I arrived, I felt happy and bouncy. However, by the time I climbed back into the car, I was subdued and miserable. At first, I thought it was due to my own emotions coming up from the session, but it was not. I had picked up the healer's energy. Beware of any healer or reader who shares too much of their personal life with you. A little drawing from their life to explain a situation is fine, for by tapping into an experience they can clarify a point. Nevertheless, if you land up counseling them, take stock. An energetic shift will be happening, usually from your aura to theirs.

Anger, fear and depression are energies that easily transfer from one person to another. We have all experienced it in our human world. You know the situations I mean. We visit someone feeling happy and light, and we leave feeling unhappy and depressed. Direct energy transfer. When working with the aura, the transfer becomes even more noticeable. Be aware of this transfer when you work or are being worked on. If your emotional state alters dramatically after the healing, you could have picked up the healer's fear, anger or depression.

If you feel this has happened to you, clear off your aura, and if possible have a cleansing salt bath. On a level, we know how our own emotions feel and this will help us recognize when we are carrying the other person's emotions. Their emotions will feel unfamiliar and somewhat confusing. When it happened to me, I felt weird and not like myself. This can be a clear sign of energy transfer.

I don't think people mean to sap us or transfer their feelings, but it does happen. I suggest that you be aware of this possible situation and clean your aura if necessary.

Levels of spiritual work

In spiritual work, everyone is working at various levels. Even though we know this instinctively, it is important to understand that we are on different planes spiritually. Some people come into the world quite psychically gifted, while others learn slowly and develop their skills over time. Unfortunately, I have noticed that jealousy can become an issue in this type of work. We can make comparisons between the skills we have and the skills others possess. I feel this jealousy and envy is a waste of energy.

Everyone is on his or her own path of spiritual development. Therefore, comparison is pointless. I have heard others enviously speak of not being able to see auras like their friend or wanting the gift another reader may have. I believe that seeing auras or hearing Spirit is not indicative of the extent of one's spiritual gift. I value the gift because of the comfort and healing it can give. It is not a magic show with tricks, bells and whistles. It is to help others, and bring peace of mind to those suffering.

Ultimately, the humbleness of the work is its greatest power. All of us have envied the skills some spiritual beings possess, but it does not mean their work is better than others. A gift is not a measure of the giving. A kind word and gentle gesture to another in need are no less important than being able to see auras or communicate with Spirit.

I wish to improve myself as a person and channel. Comparing ourselves to others will only take our focus off the real issues. Admire others and ask Spirit to help you develop a similar gift if it is in your destiny. Focus on honing a skill you would like to improve. For me, the gift came slowly and only after years of work. I did not wake up with the skills. Nor was I a child who was obviously spiritually gifted. It has taken much effort to progress to where I am now, as I had to work simultaneously on my own demons, while honing my gift.

There are advanced psychic ones who seem born with the gifts. Then there are people like me. Crucial to our development is our intention. Those who really want to help others will eventually find their path. It is all about being patient and sticking to our sacred contract to help. Before we arrived, we ticked the box labeled "sacred contract." The sacred contract stated the type of spiritual work we agreed to undertake once the time was right. Factored into this was our personal time to activate it, as well as world timing. Both times were intertwined.

Over the years, I have met many extremely gifted beings with natural skills that far outshone my ability. With their insights and healing hands, they could have done some amazing work. In spite of this, many have decided it was too hard, and they made different decisions. In my experience, it is all about the journey. Those who keep moving toward the Light can reach higher avenues of spiritual growth. It reminds me of the rabbit and the tortoise race. Slowly and surely, we can all reach our destination. With perseverance and dedication, we can visit places we never dreamt of.

Remember your sacred contract. Try to keep going, focusing on the best path for you. Admire those gifted ones, but never feel less. It is not about the actual gift. It is about what we choose to do with it and our own spiritual growth.

Asking to ascend to the next level

Our helpers are always with us, so once you are on the path remember to ask for ascension. Spirit will be very happy to support your request. Of course, we have to be patient and follow their lead. For example, if it isn't in our contract to see auras, we may never see auras. However, by asking, other doors may be opened. I began my path massaging people and never dreamt that I would be reading cards or writing books.

Keep in mind that progress might look very different to what we may have expected. My spiritual fantasy was having my own healing sanctuary in the country. Here, I saw myself walking around in a beautiful white dress, while other healers filled the rooms and all was abuzz with spiritual workers. Today, I sit quietly in my room working on a laptop closely related to a brick, writing books. The point I am making is that you need to follow the spiritual path you set out for yourself in the Garden of Remembrance. We can ask, but our contract still needs to be honored before any personal dreams. If the work seems different to what you envisaged, keep focused because you and your guides know best.

I believe this is why other people have fallen by the wayside. When they asked for particular tools or outcomes, and they did not get what they wanted, they left. If only they could have understood how it works, things might have turned out differently.

Plodding ahead has worked for me. I have been able to gather more spiritual tools and open up more of my own gifts. I believe that by surrendering to Spirit the work can climb to unimaginable places. Every day I ask to be used as a channel in the way that my guardians think is best. In doing so, their will and my will have become the same. Surrendering in this way strengthens our journey and quickens our progress.

I suggest that you admire, but not envy others. Open yourself up to Spirit and all will be as it should be. Each of us is a flower blooming in its own time. However, no bloom knows its beauty until it opens fully in God's time, in your time.

The lessening gap between the worlds

As the world's vibration quickens the gap between the dimensions lessens. If we are also ascending our vibration will increase even more, and we will be closer to the higher energies. This ascension can bring some interesting learning.

I had a very disturbing experience in a reading that highlighted the shortening gap between the dimensions. I did a reading for a lady and to me it seemed fine, until the end. When it was question time, she asked me about a couple that she knew. I saw them standing together, so I relayed the message. Then the person I was doing the reading for informed me that one of the people had actually died. Initially, I was mortified thinking I had misread.

This was a big lesson for me in relation to the energy gap between the worlds and how this may affect our readings. Luckily, my psychic friend tuned in to Spirit and I was told that the gap between the dimensions had shortened for me. In a sense, the two people were in the same space. The two worlds were now so close that I could see them simultaneously, one overlapping the other.

As you ascend your readings might suffer the same outcome. You may come to a point when you cannot clearly distinguish whether the people are in this dimension or another.

Remember, we are reading the energy fields, so they exist in all dimensions. We can only read what we see. These days during a session I explain that I read the energy; therefore, the persons concerned could be here on earth or in spirit form. You might find a similar explanation will be useful in your work.

As our worlds become closer, these kinds of adjustments need to be made. All is taken care of in the spiritual world. It just takes a little longer for us to catch up on earth.

Differentiating between the messages and us

When you begin working as a reader/healer it is important to differentiate between when you say something, and when it is channeled, because your client or friend may not be able to pick up the difference. Once you begin to speak with others it can seem like everything you say is from Spirit. Frequently, during a channeling session, some of your own words or interpretations can come into the conversation as well. This can make it even more confusing.

I have a funny way of dealing with this situation. I explain when I am speaking from Spirit and when it is only me speaking.

Normally, I will say, "This is me speaking" or "This is them speaking." It stops any confusion. There is a third situation that can arise, namely, that I am unsure whether the message is coming from Spirit or me. Occasionally, I can't distinguish. I am as honest as I can be because there have been times that I could not separate the messages.

People think it is strange when I voice these three types of communications. However, over the years they have proven to be an excellent way to channel. Although it sounds funny when I say, "Oh, this is me talking" I believe that everyone benefits. I have found the messages can "slip" into normal conversations; therefore, I need a way to identify them. I always know when it's the angels because I don't "think" the sentence. I begin to speak and feel like an observer when I relay it. Generally, I think how smart or beautiful the wording was.

Once we begin to be clear about when we are talking or channeling everything in life becomes easier. People need to know when we are speaking as a concerned friend or as a channel. I am sure using this type of explanation will help you, your friends and clients. As always, there is a solution to every problem in the spiritual world. We only need to have the knowledge and awareness to find it.

Reading energy

When people do a reading or healing, they tap into the person's energy. On a daily level, people tap into the aura. They can read energy and will sense if others are upset or ill. When their friend says they are fine, they know there is more going on. We read each other every day on an energetic level.

Having said that, I do feel that the way we tap in can advance or limit our work. A good medium or psychic reads the aura in a different manner. Of course, we can also tap into the aura like everyone else, but a skilled channel reads "through" into the energy body. It is like instead of reading the surface of the aura; we read deep into the aura through space and time. This is a multidimensional reading, like looking deep into the pond, not only the surface. Once we begin to read in this way much more information can come through. This is the skill that differentiates accurate, high level readings/healings from the others. It is the depth of the work that affects the quality of the channel.

An advanced channel will not be restricted to the human condition. They will read from the soul energy. You might be told about a new car or trip overseas when you are being read on a human energy level, but if your reader is advanced, the information will delve into soul issues like paths, karma and past lives influencing this life.

Most people are drawn to the reader/healer that vibrates at their level. If the channeled information is unsatisfying for the client, there are reasons. One reason is that the work was at an inappropriate level. Maybe the work was far beyond what the person was ready to hear, or it did not tackle the issues they wanted to address. It does not mean the readings were poor. It has to do with the reader/healer matching the person.

As a reader/healer it took me time to work out where I fitted in the bigger picture. Instinctively, I knew my readings were unlike many others. I did not get the color of the new car or the names of the dead people. I relayed information about soul development and past lives. I connected to deceased ones, but in another way. I can get the extra human messages, and so I regularly leave a section at the end of the session where the person can ask any question not yet covered. If we don't get all the answers, it is okay. In fact, it can be very good. Probably Spirit is making the person work through a particular lesson.

People normally come with their own agenda. Remember, we are merely the channels. We can only channel what we are given. Stand in the truth and all will be well.

Information being blocked

During your sessions, don't feel bad if you can't get the information you need or that someone requests. Just know that in the world of Spirit, it happens like that sometimes. There are several reasons. Of course, there are times when we can't access it. Maybe, we aren't in the right space, or we have to wait for clarity. We may have no answer initially, and yet hours or days later the message pops into our head. Be aware that quite often there is no answer because it has not yet been decided. Therefore, the outcome is still unclear. Free will is typically the reason.

On some occasions, no answer is provided. In these cases, the person needs to work it out, for it might be their lesson to sort out. So, if we give them the answer, their lesson will be lost. It can feel weird to receive no answer. Psychically, it can feel like we are looking into a void.

Another situation can happen when Spirit doesn't want any interference. On occasion, particular things need to be put in place for a reason. It takes the spiritual world ages to set up events and meetings. If information were relayed it could affect the desired outcomes, and so as a reader you won't be allowed to tap in. It will be blocked.

These situations can be challenging. Firstly, your lack of information can be frustrating, and not being able to tune in may be a new experience for you. Secondly, once the situation has turned out the way it needed to, others may want to question your skills as a channel. There is always some clown who knows little about how the system works who may want to challenge you. Over the years, I have heard countless, smart comments attacking the spiritual work. I simply ignore them or make a joke back. It is pointless to try and explain the ins and outs of these spiritual procedures to some wise guy. These days I deal with it quickly and calmly. If pressed, I explain it was exactly the way it was supposed to be, and normally that puts an end to it.

On a personal level, I can see why blocking has occurred. I will be able to see why my best friend married someone I did not pick as being untrustworthy. She was supposed to learn her lessons with him so the information was blocked. It is not my fault that I could not read him until it was too late. Even then, if I had warned her, she was in no mood to listen. It was exactly how it was meant to be.

Still, as long as we understand why it turned out a particular way, it does not matter what others make of it. These situations can put us out of kilter with others, but it is a small price to pay for a wonderful gift.

In general, people want an answer; however, never make something up, especially if you are pressured. Be honest and direct. I have literally told people that it is for them to find out. They might not like it. However, it is important they understand their part in the process. In the long run, by being honest you will retain your integrity, and they will come to trust your word.

Being wrong sometimes

As with all things, sometimes we will be wrong. It is the way of the world. Some of the most incredible healers and psychics have experienced this situation. There are times it just happens. It could be your interpretation was wrong or a mistake was made for another reason. Don't focus on it, merely accept it and move on. It is very important that we don't allow doubt to affect our work because doubt can block our ability to channel clearly. As long as you do the best you can, what more can you ask?

I know that other people can make you feel uncomfortable when your relay was wrong. While other messages you have given them were clear and accurate, they will focus on your only mistake and not remember all the other information.

It takes courage to accept error and not let it stop you working. Move on and don't dwell on it. Not all is perfect here on earth. Why should your channeling be any different? Focus on all the good work you can do with Spirit, while allowing for some imperfections.

Static on the channel

The basic difference between an exceptional reader/healer and a poor one is their ability to tune into the channel properly. Communicating clearly is paramount to a good outcome. A clear, direct line to Spirit will make for excellent work, while any fuzziness will alter and compromise the read. I work on getting the best line available. This means being focused and listening with our soul ears because the human always puts its own slant on any message coming through.

By doing major bodywork, you can clear yourself as a channel. That means eating carefully, exercising and minimizing bad habits, such as drugs, smoking or too much alcohol, because a clear aura makes for a clearer read.

There are many people engaged in psychic work at this point in our world development. Many of them are not exactly on the channel, so to speak. Maybe they can receive some accurate information but frequently, or in some cases most of the time, they are not able to receive clearly. I refer to this situation as static on the line, because, even though they think that they are always on the channel, they aren't. Often, they believe everything they receive is correct. Sometimes it is, mostly it is not.

Static blurs the real message. With parts missing the interpretation is compromised. This on/off approach will not be useful. Some messages will come true, and others will turn out very differently. These readers/healers can struggle with recognizing which parts of their interpretations are right and which parts are not. Static creates enormous problems for psychic work.

If you think you are experiencing these problems work at clearing your aura and strengthening your connection to your guides. Remember that static can occur when we are emotionally upset or ill. Fatigue will also blur the reception, as our focus is not there.

An accurate, clear channel is a blessing, while a statically-challenged one creates more problems and confusion. If you encounter a channel experiencing static, learn to be discerning. If you are on the receiving end, your instincts should kick in and help you to pick up what is a real message and what is not. I believe that the messages should "feel" right and resonate with you.

Static can happen to any of us at any time. No one is immune from static problems. If more people were aware of static and understood when it was occurring it would be invaluable, for by seeing it, we could make the necessary adjustments. We could also see it in others and be more discerning about their messages.

Static can be a temporary or a permanent feature. Some psychics only encounter static rarely, while others have major problems. Generally, the last group is often unaware of it and thinks everything they channel is correct. If they encounter much failure in their messages, they rarely address the static issue. It is always put down to something else.

I believe that one good message or healing is better than many inaccurate and poor ones. These days, if I can't get clarity, I see it as a positive sign of my growth. At least, I can see the clear days and the unclear ones.

Once we acknowledge the existence of static on the channel, we have made much spiritual growth. For in understanding its existence, we can become more accurate light workers.

Blocking the healing/reading

There is a strange situation that can arise when we do the work. It can be blocked. I have had this happen to me and found it quite unsettling. In these cases, the block will come from the other person. Nevertheless, recognizing this type of block can take experience. Blocking happens occasionally. It has to do with not wanting or being ready to hear the message, and it can operate on many layers.

The most common one is when the person verbalizes that they want to be healed, but on a deeper level set up a block. We have all met these individuals. They tell us they want to be better, but block every attempt to make changes. I recognize this pattern due to one curious behavior. They always want someone other than themselves to heal them, to fix it all up. My warning bells begin to ring in these situations. Not wanting to fix it themselves indicates to me that they have a painful block they don't want to address. Whenever we want another person to do our work, we are blocking our own growth.

Blocking can happen when we do a reading or a healing. I can literally feel them blocking. It feels like a wall. I will be talking or working on them, and as I do, I can feel the wall go up. It's like your words and energy are being shut out. Everyone will have his or her own particular way of sensing the block. It is beneficial to work out how your aura signals to you.

Once the block goes up, I stop trying to connect and change the subject. If you keep going it can get very uncomfortable. I have known people to begin arguments during the work in an effort to keep the block in place. If this happens, know you have overstepped the line and understand how close to the problem you are. Remember, not everyone is ready to tackle his or her issues.

Timing is important. I try not to push buttons when I receive a blocking response. Sometimes, we are there as healers just to open the door a little. Maybe, when the person is ready, the door can open more. It is always about them. We are only the channels.

The saying, "The lady doth protest too much" is valid in this blocking area. You will find people telling you things are great when you know otherwise. It is where they need to be, so keep quiet. Later, they may face their blocks, but it needs to be when they are ready.

In these instances, we will know our message is correct, even if they tell us we are wrong. Ultimately, being right is not what it is all about. We are there to assist them if they are ready to deal with it. Never push or confront. Normally, there can be much pain and sadness behind blocks, and it will take great strength and courage to feel these repressed emotions again.

Respect a person's decision to block. Try not to defend your message or labor the point, and allow the person space. If they begin to argue, don't argue back. Just say it is what you felt, and suggest that perhaps you will both have more clarity later. Remember that a person trying to hold down a painful block can be formidable. It's never about being right. It's about being respectful and kind. Under all the blocking, the soul knows the truth; sometimes the human part of us just isn't ready to hear it.

Another aspect of this work is the amount of progress people can do. With some, the healing can only go so far. Once they encounter the hard areas or new blocks, they can stall or revert to the start. We can feel sad about it, but never see it as a failure. It signals how far ahead we have both come. To heal means to face and work on your own issues. A good healer can help to guide you, but it is the person who actually allows the deeper healing to occur.

Healing is never static or that easy, and contrary to opinion, not everyone wants to be healed. It is complex, and frequently perplexing. People may say they want to heal, but in reality, they are not ready. Knowing this aspect of the work will make the whole process easier for you. To be healed, we have to take personal responsibility. Not everyone can do that.

As a healer, do not despair. The healing is always given. The receiving of the healing lies at the person's feet, and they will decide. We are only responsible for doing the healing, being the channel. Never take on board the outcome for it will always be their outcome, their choice.

Argumentative clients

You might have already experienced argumentative clients. I have found it can be disconcerting to try to work with these individuals. No matter how experienced we are, an arguing client is a pain.

Channeling is like starting the water running. The information begins to flow, and we are off. I believe the deeper the read, the stronger the flow. Therefore, when someone begins to argue, it breaks the flow and disrupts the speed and depth of the read. Essentially, arguing is a control issue. For by arguing the person is trying to control the reading or healing. Spirit can hit a sore point, a place of truth. A place the recipient might not want to go. When this happens, my advice is to ask for more information or clarity. For example, if you say the person is a perfectionist, and they disagree, ask Spirit to be clearer. I always stand by what I am given. I mean, if given the choice of listening to another human or an advanced spiritual being, I know who I would choose to listen to. In addition, Spirit always sees the truth.

Unfortunately, once people begin to disagree with you, it can affect the rest of the reading. This is where you need to make some decisions. You have rights as well. If it becomes too stressful to work you can stop. Charge them accordingly, and wave them good-bye. Even so, be aware that this approach can become confrontational. Control freaks don't like the shift of power.

Unless told otherwise, I continue with the reading. I feel that they have come for a reason, and Spirit may have a bigger plan than I can see. The stop/start aspect is hard, but a good learning for you. Persevering can also have some unusual outcomes. In my experience, I have regularly felt the person softening towards the end of the session.

Channeling in this fashion is tiring. I recommend you decide whether you wish to read them again. I had a very difficult woman recently. I soldiered on. When she left, I decided I had done my part spiritually. I have free will too. Next time, if there is one, I may suggest she might want to find another reader.

Learning to read someone who tries to control the reading is hard, but it has some valuable lessons. Although we work with Spirit, we have equal rights. Implement them when needed. Ultimately, our readings and healings should be joyous and uplifting experiences.

Taking their energy with them

An unusual practice can happen with some people we work on. It happens mostly with healing work. In this situation, you and your spiritual helpers will do the required healing. However, as the person goes to leave, they will collect the "removed" energy and take it with them.

In my years of work, I have seen people reset their aura. Even so, dragging their energy out with them as they left was a surprise to me. It came to my attention due to my parting words. I ended one of my sessions by suggesting that they leave it all behind, and in doing so, Spirit would take care of it. With those words, the reality of what was happening energetically became apparent.

Often, we have carried some energy for so long that we can feel almost naked without it. It has become part of who we are. Therefore, after a healing session, our first instinct may be to collect it and take it with us when we leave. In my experience, despite the warning, many could not help but take it with them; it is like their security blanket.

In mentioning this phenomenon, I don't wish to judge these actions. Nevertheless, as healers, it is useful information for us too. On a personal level, it may prevent us from collecting our energy at the conclusion of our own healing session.

In our world of free will Spirit will never intervene. Neither should we. Still, I think by alerting the person to this practice at least they have a chance to make another choice. As they say, when we know better, we do better.

On different channels

It can happen that we can visit a healer or reader and have an unsuccessful outcome. Normally, this is because we are vibrating differently to them. There are many advanced souls on earth. The rule of thumb is that the higher energy flows to the lower one. So if we are trying to be healed by someone who is vibrating lower than we are, then they may receive the flow of energy from us.

We can also experience a reader, who has trouble reading us. They can tell us they think we are blocking. Blocking does happen, but in this situation, it won't be the reason. My husband went for a reading and had this problem. When it came time to be read the lady couldn't read him at all. Initially, she thought he was blocking, but he wasn't. Then she asked if he was psychic. On some level, she was aware his vibration was the issue. Due to her fear, she could not do the reading. I believe her fear of working with him shut down her own abilities.

The young souls on earth at this time are vibrating at phenomenal rates. They outshine most of us and for them to find readers and healers can be a challenge. This does not mean we can't work on these people. There is a solution. When I am working on one of these souls, I am instructed by my guides to raise my vibration before they arrive. Only then can I start the work.

There is another reason the reading or healing will not work. It may not be good to be worked on by particular persons, as their channeled energies may not sit well with our auras. Perhaps the two energies can't blend. This type of situation will feel very strange. You will not feel comfortable throughout the session, and the whole thing may not flow easily. You can leave feeling quite unsatisfied. Frequently, this is a clash of energies, not necessarily a vibrational rate discrepancy. I am very careful about who works on me. I know it sounds weird, but unless it feels right, I can't do it.

Healings and readings are frequently about the right timing. It has to be the best time for the person. As a channel,

I will never talk anyone into coming for work. I believe that their soul always knows the best time for them.

There are many types of energy work. This is good. We all come from various backgrounds and carry unique energy patterns. Not all energy work suits everyone. Personally, I prefer the angelic realm; it is where I feel safe and comfortable. This energy works well for me because it comes from love. Some people are drawn to universal light. These days this kind of energy work is popular. Reiki has taken off and opened doors to other healing work. Magnetic healing is also available.

There are many shamans here to assist Mother Earth. These people possess skills concerning the earth and the animal kingdom. Some connect to the spirits of nature, including fairies and nature spirits. There is much focus on acknowledging these other energies and respecting each living group. Spirit animals feature regularly in these healing cultures. In this century, there are many Native American souls here as well as some who originate from South America and Egypt. These shamans bring with them ancient skills and practices, and by tapping into their soul; they can open doors of healing and prophecy.

Another popular energy work is witchcraft. I remember someone coming for healing work. The session went well and afterwards, we chattered away. I showed my ignorance when the lady started talking about an interest of hers. She told me how she studied "wicker." That was how I heard it. I went on about all the cane baskets I had made and the challenge of keeping the wet cane in control. Of course, she looked at me strangely. Wicca and wicker—two different worlds.

I like God and the angels. Their energy works well for me. However, in evolving as a reader or healer you must decide where your place lies.

Heaven-sent Healing

Send love and healing even when the person seems unable to receive. It will sit quietly until the soul is ready to draw it unto itself. Love sent is never wasted.

How to send absent healing

Being able to send absent healing is a wonderful gift, and everyone can send healing. I believe that we all have our own way to work our magic. Some people send in a general sense, while others send very selectively. My world, like yours, can become quite busy, and during these times, I use the general send process. With this method, I think of the person and project a large amount of healing light to them. It is quick, and I know their aura will sort out where it goes. You can also ask spiritual helpers to work on them. Both methods will ensure the healing light reaches them.

I think that it is always good to send the healing more than once. Initially, I set up a thoughtform to do this work. I make the healing intention that every time I think of the person, the healing energy is attached to the thought, and then it automatically goes to them. It is amazing how often we think of some people in one week. With this intention in place, I know the healing light goes to them. This is automatic healing at its best.

Another way is to be more specific. For instance, if your recipient has a sore, left knee, visualize the person's knee and project the energy there. This direct send can be done over and over again. You can flood the area with healing light and know that their soul will use it wisely. Energy is never wasted. If there is any residual energy, it will be stored away for another time. All of us can hold energy reserves in our aura. Just as we can store minerals or extra fat around the body, so we can store excess energy. It is like our built-in energy insurance.

In serious cases, or when I need to work more deeply, I use a more honed healing. I see the person in front of me. In my mind, they are facing me and by focusing, I direct the healing light to the required place. It could be to their right hip, bad knee or sore back. Sometimes, if I have the feeling that they need a particular color, like gold or red, I direct it there. Perhaps you can use a laser method or any other intuitive way to affect the healing. This is a useful way to fill a depleted or sick place in the aura.

If you find it difficult to visualize, then use a tangible object to represent the person. It could be a teddy, doll or a pillow. I suggest that you work on the object like it is simply the person. This method works well when you first start absent healing as the object creates an interface between you and the other world. It gives you a more tangible focus.

Once the healing has begun, I focus until I think it is finished. Next, I ask the healing light to keep working for as long as it is needed. By setting in place the last intention, we can stop working and allow the spiritual work to finish in Spirit time. Of course, people always have the right to receive or not, and we need to be aware of this with all healing endeavors.

As with all healing once you have finished, disconnect by washing your aura and cutting the cords from you and the other person. Remember, Spirit has it all in hand now.

Absent healing is wonderful when life is suddenly turned upside down. When tragedies occur, we all pray for help, even the usual non-believers send out a cry for help. However, in the midst of chaos people can't always see that help has been delivered. I usually know when the family has put out the call. Normally, I get told about the accident, and know I have to do my absent healing work. So I quietly get on with it. At these times, the family will be unaware of the work being done, but all will be revealed at some other time.

I had a situation like this recently. An acquaintance of ours had suffered a terrible motorbike crash and was not expected to survive. I was guided to do absent healing. After a few weeks, I posted a get-well card and mentioned that I had been doing absent healing. I knew the family would not really understand all the work that was being done spiritually. When I mentioned the healing, I was speaking to their soul. I did not want any thanks. The message was to convey to the family that their prayers were being answered within the spiritual world.

We can also use absent healing when someone is suffering from stress or emotional upset. By and large, the emotions involved are anger, fear or depression. Absent healing will assist in lessening these feelings.

I have had people come to me years later and give thanks. When all the dust settled, they could see clearly, but it is a rare thing. Do the work with no expectation. Some who have crossed over may visit us to give their thanks. I have "psychically" heard their words of gratitude long after they had passed away. One or two visited me in dreams looking well and vibrant. A big change from how they looked on earth.

Occasionally, the angels will let us know the work is reaching others. We may be told how the doctors can't understand how the person survived and is still alive, but we will know why. However, repeatedly our work will go unnoticed in our physical plane. I accept it is the nature of absent healing.

I love absent healing. It can be done anywhere and at anytime. We can cross time and space and send healing all over the dimensions. Furthermore, nothing stops us from sending healing to special loved ones on the other side.

Enjoy the gift of giving. Once you find your own way of sending, it will advance your own progress spiritually. Like with all things, the more we do, the better we become. Although you will not always get much feedback on earth, you and Spirit will know all has been sent in love and good faith.

Healings held in time

Sometimes people want the healing, but can't receive it at the time. In these conditions, it can be "saved." The healing is held at their doorstep until they may be ready to open up and let it in. It could be the next day, or three lifetimes ahead.

Nothing sent is ever wasted because energy can never be destroyed. Therefore, if we ask Spirit to send healing to someone, and we see no signs of change here, don't lose heart. The healing will be there waiting to be activated. It can be disappointing to see no results, but we are not in control of the healing. All we can do is to ask for it to be sent.

It is the action of asking that will help to set the "healing" wheels in motion. Faith plays a large part in this kind of work. No one can prove it, and we can't always understand universal truths. They just are as they are. Don't measure your success in worldly outcomes. Measure your success in your pure intention to help another person or creature.

Unusual absent healing

I had an interesting experience last year. It involved sending absent healing in a real physical space. It happened at the dentist. After my appointment, I was in the office waiting to pay the bill, and a very scared lady was sitting there. She hadn't been able to visit the dentist for twenty years, and she was petrified. I began to tell her how caring and gentle the dentist was, and during this conversation, I saw Spirit showing me what they wanted me to do. I was guided to give her healing. They instructed me to visualize my hand extending out and being placed on her heart. By putting my energetic hand on her heart, the calming, healing light could be channeled into her aura. So I stood there chatting away, while I put my energetic hand on her heart. It was a beautiful moment. As I was about to leave, I asked that my energetic hand be there for as long as she needed it.

I had never worked on someone so directly in a public place. While my soul did the light work, the human soothed her with words. Wow! Obviously, the lady was able to receive and had probably asked for help before she arrived. What struck me was the power of the moment. I had been shown another way to project instant healing in normal human circumstances. I believe if you are supposed to work in this way it will be channeled to you. You will see a visual and quietly do the work.

Since then I have not felt compelled to operate in this fashion when out and about. It seemed like a special situation which was probably set up by others on the other side. Its simplicity and beauty were amazing.

If you are called to give healing in this way remember, you are simply the channel. A greater power will guide where the healing goes.

Asking guardians to work on us or others

It is quite okay to ask Spirit to work on others or us. There have been times I was too tired or preoccupied to work on myself. At those times, I asked to be worked on as I lay quietly on my bed or during sleep. I noticed that when Spirit work on us in this way we can generally feel the energy moving around our aura. Frequently, it can feel like something is crawling on our head, hands or back. The sensations are weird and hard to describe. Spirit can lift off and fill the aura like we do in healings. They just work at a higher level, and I suspect, with more focus. Therefore, what may take us one hour could be done in seconds. The energy is very dense on earth, but Spirit is vibrating at a much higher rate. The amount of energy they can send is infinite, and unlimited by time and space. In these circumstances, it is like humans have the small hosepipe to work with, while Spirit has the enormous one. Having no rules around space and time, they can cross many dimensions.

When we work, we reach up vibrationally to connect to Spirit, and at the same time, Spirit needs to vibrate down to us. There has to be a drop in vibrational rate to accommodate the healing. We are enclosed in a physical body, and we can only channel as high as the physical body can cope with. If we do a lot of work on ourselves, we can raise our vibrational rate, but it will never be as high as Spirit.

I feel asking Spirit to work on us, another person or an animal is a very empowering act of faith.

Sending healing and love on a grand scale

Every night, and frequently during the day, I send light and love to particular people; I enjoy doing it. Over the years, I have found that the number of people I have been sending healing to have steadily increased.

I have also experienced other ways to send healing to many people. In healing circles the people's names are placed in a dish and the healing sent to those in the bowl. In other circles, they use a book to write their names in.

In spite of this, I felt that I was missing something. Then it occurred to me that it was the energetic link. Energy attracts energy, and I began to recognize the most important part of the process was the energy connection. I began to experiment with this factor. After some reflection, I visualized an energy wall, a wall of vibrating energy. Next, I put my people onto the wall. In this way, they were permanently attached, in a very nice way, onto the wall connecting to the energy. If you wished to use a bowl, you would energize the entire bowl and the empty space inside it. If it were a floor, you would energize the floor. Once your energy base is constructed, you can place your people onto or into the area. As usual, I place them in the space with their soul approval to receive or not. Always respect another's choices.

Today, the energy wall works well for me. I can expand the wall as needed, and clearly see everyone I am sending to. It was a relief to find a quicker way to reach everyone. I had solved the memory game I played at eleven o'clock at night of trying to figure out whom I may have missed. Everyone had their space and received the light whenever I connected to the wall.

The method you use to connect to the wall is important. It must sit comfortably with you. Initially, I visualized my hands in front of me sending the healing light and love toward the wall. With this process, I was consciously channeling energy into the wall. In doing so, the energy traveled along the wall and fed everyone with healing and love. It was wonderful. No one missed out and all received a good hit every time I visualized it. I could also do the work in seconds. It could be on the way to town, on the bus, during a shower, or in the few minutes that I had free. The more that I held my visual hands out and connected to the energy of the wall, the easier it became. At first, I constructed my wall with those closest to me and over the months more people have been added. The limitless nature of the process is fabulous.

I discovered my wall had another benefit. Some relationships are difficult. There can be people in our lives who have hurt us terribly. These emotional problems can compromise our ability to send healing and love. Nevertheless, the energy wall made it easier for me to pop them on regardless of the past, and once they were on the wall; I just kept sending the energy. Given time, by constantly sending love and light to these difficult ones, I believe that we can become closer to forgiving them. The act of healing may even shift the blocks between us, and we may find our peace in the here and now. Moreover, the healing work would have already begun before we crossed over to the other side. This process can burn much karma as well.

Once I hooked into this way of absent healing, I felt a sense of relief and coming "home." In the act of giving, I felt my spiritual journey was advantaged. For the most part, few people will know how much is being done behind the scenes. Don't let this worry you. All in the universe see this silent spiritual work. Although many can't fully understand the spiritual work being done, be assured that once these people cross, all will be revealed. For now, we will have to do it with no expectations, only good intentions and love.

I enjoy my energy wall. Every day it becomes better and better. Feel free to put animals, pets and plants into your energy place. You can put the planets, the seas and mountains there as well. Not everyone on your wall has to be alive. I added my beloved Golden Retriever who is in heaven and some old friends who aren't with me anymore. I encourage you to follow your instincts. I believe once in place, the energy wall will last for as long as necessary.

There is no reason why you can't put your spiritual self on the wall and send yourself love and healing too. How cool is that? How amazing will the work be? If you wish, you can send the energy wall different colored lights and blessings. I love my wall. Every time that I connect it becomes more beautiful and rich with healing light, love and colors. I think when I pass; I will take it with me.

The most important learning I received about this method was the energy connection. By energizing the bowl, wall, floor or construct, we allow the light to cross from us to it. This is fundamental to its wonderful success. In the past, I had worked with the bowl idea where we placed people's names in it and sent healing light. However, I always felt that somehow that something else was needed. It was the energetic connection.

I hope you have fun designing your own energy healing structure and sending light and love.

Absent earth healing

Everything is speeding up on earth. Countless beings have been working quietly to lift the vibration of the world, for Mother Earth has needed much love and light to get her through this fragile time. All the prayers and gifts of love and light have enabled her to make shifts and to cleanse. The increase in weather changes like fires, floods and earthquakes all point to the changes occurring and the need for more spiritual work. Quietly, in our homes many of us have been sending aid to the animals, seas, lands and air. All these healings to the earth have strengthened her.

There has been the physical manifestation of the healing at work. Groups to save endangered species and protect animals have increased, while environmental concerns are being addressed. Disasters have been lessened, and weather changes have been averted because of the healing work being sent. We can all heal our world merely by focusing and sending love and healing light to troubled areas. It is unnecessary to leave our homes. Frequently, I have watched the news, seen the problem and immediately sent light and healing to the place or people. Can you imagine how much we could all do to assist in our world by these simple acts?

The beauty of it all is that when we manifest it first in the higher energies, it eventually filters down into our physical world.

Never underestimate the power of change coming from united soul work.

Soul rescue

There are many skilled light workers who can do soul rescue. They help others in crossing to the other side. Particularly, during world catastrophes, they assist those in passing over or those who are lost. For the most part, the people who are engaged in this type of work do it quietly and rarely speak about it. It is an instinctive response from them, a learned knowing from past lives.

After world disasters there can be confusion. If people die in a traumatic way, they can become confused, and some will not know that they are actually dead. Sudden death can disorientate them. In these circumstances, they can become lost between the worlds. When light workers send love and light to all of those who have passed, it supports these people in their crossing. The light and love sent helps them cross, making it easier for Spirit to collect them.

Another type of soul rescue concerns those spirits referred to as ghosts. Typically, they are lost souls that no longer have enough light to cross and may have to frequent the earth through time and space. Light sent enables them to go home. Some children can get caught between the dimensions. Children on earth regularly see them in their spiritual form. Spirit children are very attracted to human children. We can send love and light to help these souls to cross. However, I still believe that only those who wish to go will do so.

I know that all these healings we do assist the universe. You don't have to be a Reiki master or skilled healer to do it. Everyone can do this work and help in healing our planet.

Love is love, light is light and, in the universe, all is the Oneness.

Magical Healing Pendulums

We are all healers so remember that our healing intentions reach all. Given time, even the closed ones will receive the gift being sent.

Using the pendulum

The pendulum is a valuable tool in healing work because it shows us how the energy is working around the body. You can use a glass, crystal or wood pendulum. Choose one that resonates with you. Then it is playtime. Everyone has to use the pendulum the way that is right for him/her for it will be his or her instrument. When I was first given one, I had to find out what I could use it for.

I was told it would act as my eyes, and by observing its spin, I could see movement of energy. This is how I work. I hold the pendulum over the body and wait for it to begin to spin. For me, it goes clockwise when the energy is flowing in a positive way. When the aura is releasing or unbalanced, it goes backwards. If there is a problem, it can swing back and forth, while a still pendulum indicates blocked or stagnant energy.

In addition, I use the pendulum to move the energy. By holding the pendulum over a part of the body, for example a chakra, the energy can be balanced. When I work, I let it start moving and wait for it to stop. This can take from a few seconds to an hour or more.

The reason the pendulum works is because it connects your energy field to the energy field of the person you are working on. If the person is tired, I can feel it by the way the pendulum swings; it will feel heavy. I can feel pain being released coming up from the pendulum. The more you use it and find out your own method, the better it becomes.

No one works in the same manner as we come from different lives and learning. Therefore, I encourage you to read the pendulum in your own way. Keep in mind that there is no right or wrong method. Work in the way that you feel comfortable with. Follow your own path.

By using the pendulum we can work on people, on animals and ourselves. It is amazing to see that pendulum whizzing around a sore knee, and then eventually settle down and stop. During the time, you may feel sensations and pain in your hand or body, while the pendulum does its thing.

When I am working and using the pendulum for healing, I wait until the pendulum stops swinging and becomes still. Sometimes, it can take ages, so be patient. If the pain begins to run into your hand or up your arm, keep the pendulum there. It is very important not to disconnect when the energy is moving and to allow the energy body to come into balance. Like hands-on healing, the pain releasing from the body can be extremely strong. It amazes me how much pain one aura can hold. If you are working on yourself, you may feel it as well. As the pain is released from the aura it often makes its presence felt. When the aura is releasing it is as if we are dragging the unwanted energy out by a rope. As it is pulled through the aura, we may feel it moving. These sensations are usually a new experience in our human world.

Frequently, the person we are working on will feel the pain before we do. When I begin to feel it too, I tell them, and we can rejoice in its release. Typically, when this healing occurs people express relief that the pain has gone. During healings people have immediately thanked Spirit for taking it away. In speaking and acknowledging its departure, much healing occurs. Spirit, the person and you as the channel are all working in the same space. The power is threefold with this combined approach.

If you don't feel any pain, don't worry. Usually, some pain is felt, but not always. These days I sense when feeling the pain is unnecessary. Maybe I am being protected or the person receiving the healing does not need any "proof" in the form of pain. In some healing circles the lack of the pain is supposed to indicate that we are working at a higher level spiritually.

Personally, I believe healing is individual and unique, and as a result, each healing will be what it needs to be, regardless of our human spin on it.

In some sessions, I have found that particular pains can't be released without being felt. It depends on each individual situation. If you feel the pain, deal with it. If the person feels it, explain the release pattern. If no one feels pain, be happy. Try not to be confined to any particular dogma. Spirit always knows best. Some pains are so terrible that I feel that we are protected from feeling them. Therefore, not feeling the pain does not indicate that there wasn't a release.

Occasionally, by feeling the pain, the other person's plight is recognized by the healer too. I worked on a beautiful man with throat cancer. When I was releasing the pain, it was excruciating. Both, he and I had tears in our eyes. I was praying for the pain to go for him and for me. It made me appreciate the incredible suffering that he was experiencing at the time. In a sense, through the healing sessions, we had forged a special bond, a common understanding of his pain.

Another aspect of using the pendulum is when it stops spinning, and you think the healing is complete, but it starts swinging again. In these circumstances, the energy is coming off the aura in layers. One layer has to be removed, only to uncover another. Keep in mind that the place you think you are working on is not always where the energy is being affected. Just because you are holding the pendulum over the knee or heart does not indicate the work is there. The pendulum may be releasing unwanted energies from the toes or lower back. If you are unsure ask your recipient because generally, the person can sense and tell us where they feel the energy moving. Never underestimate the way Spirit work. While we think we are healing their knee, we may be really working on their kidneys.

I trust that the higher beings know best. If you tune in you can normally be told where the work is being done. It can be a surprise to find out the knee you are working on will not be healed during this session. If there is a more pressing area, it will take precedence. Many times people will present with one problem, only to receive healing somewhere else. This specialized work may stop them from getting seriously ill. Your guardians and theirs decide upon this action. In these cases, their knee could continue to hurt, and they may view the healing as a failure. As the channel you will just have to wear it. It's all right. We don't have to prove anything in these situations. If we did explain it, what good would it do? By telling them they were going to get seriously ill we could create more fear, and we all know how damaging fear is to the aura.

For the most part, people want the easy fix. Be comforted you understand the importance of the real work that has been performed and know that now they may have an opportunity to avoid a life-threatening disease. I feel a sore knee that is not healed is a small price to pay.

These days I know when these "silent" healings occur, and I honor Spirit. While your client does not understand now, all will be revealed once they cross. Nothing is ever wasted.

The pendulum is a powerful tool in healing work. Trust that Spirit will guide you when you use it, and embrace the healing it can bring.

The individual path

Although the pendulum can give us an accurate measure of energy, you need to work out how the shape is for you. Remember that the pattern of the pendulum will be a combination of your energy, the other person and your spiritual helpers. When I use the pendulum, it swings around in very large circles. In general, I have noticed that my pendulum circles are much bigger than others. For example, when my husband uses the pendulum, it swings with a much smaller circle when checking the same thing.

Recently, I had validation of the various pendulum swing sizes at a Reiki group. Spirit had instructed me to use my pendulum to check the chakras. There was a rather controlling man there. During the session, he directed everyone like he was the boss. Once I began to use my pendulum, the Reiki boss began to challenge me. He told me I was making the pendulum swing with my hands, and he refused to accept my method was correct and honest. I explained to him that it was just the way the pendulum worked in my hands, but he carried on about it being wrong. I knew he was unable to encompass individual differences; nevertheless, his narrow view was upsetting, especially in a group situation. Needless to say, my visits to the Reiki group confirmed my thoughts about people's different outcomes when using the pendulum.

All you have to work out is how your hand uses the pendulum because each pendulum responds to the individuals concerned. Never allow another to tell you how it has to work. Find your own method and follow your own guidance. Everyone heals in his or her own way. We are all healers in our own right.

Absent healing using the pendulum

The pendulum can also be used for absent healing. I can use it to "see" how someone's chakras are when they are not in my physical presence. You can clear their chakras using a pendulum in this fashion. Of course, working in this space requires concentrated mind focus, and it may take you time to perfect the skill. If you can't achieve any movement at first, be patient, and with practice, you may. Absent healing via the pendulum can balance a wobbly chakra anywhere in the world.

This is the way I work. I put the pendulum over my left hand (palm up) and ask to see the chakra. Once the pendulum begins to move, I work on the person like they are in front of me. This is one of the ways that I send healing absently. All it takes is a quiet place, intention and mental concentration. I can feel all the tingling, pain and heat, just like when I am working on the person in the physical world. It is an amazing experience!

When I first tried to refine this gift, I checked it physically. I would check my husband or son with the pendulum. Then I would go away and absently work on the unbalanced place. On returning, I would check the chakras or troubled spots again with the pendulum. It was exciting to see how the absent pendulum healing actually worked. My little experiment proved I was doing what I thought I was doing. Great validation!

We don't have to be limited to the chakras. The whole aura is moving energy. The pendulum can unblock, release excess energy or feed an under-energized area.

Therefore, if the person can tell us where the problem is, then we can focus and work there. Great healing can be sent using the pendulum. Time and distance make no difference. All we have to do is hold the pendulum and focus. With practice, the process becomes quicker and easier. Often, I do the surrounding areas on the person to check that I have not missed a contributing problem. For example, with a headache, I do the third eye, the crown, back of the head and the back of the neck.

The more we work with the pendulum, the more effective our healings become. I believe that by doing absent healing with this method that we can extend our abilities as a healing channel.

Types of pendulums

In the books, I have read many people express rigid beliefs concerning the use of pendulums. I suggest you follow your own instincts.

Although particular pendulums are recommended, I can simply take off a necklace and use that. I don't agree with many of the rules and regulations concerning their use. The most important thing is to feel comfortable using whatever you choose. I can use anything around including glass, crystal or wood. It is all about sending the energy, not just the instrument.

Remember, your intention is greater than the material of the pendulum. Sometimes, I have been guided to use a particular pendulum. Perhaps, their aura needs the rose quartz pendulum, or the earthiness of a wooden one. Follow your feelings and use what you intuitively know is best.

Spirit will guide us when cleaning is necessary. I clean my crystal ones with a salt-water mix. Some people like to bury their pendulums in the earth, while others place them in the moonlight. We can hold the pendulum in our hand and channel cleansing light through it too. Cleansing is an individual choice. Do what feels right at the time.

Contrary to some opinions, it is your choice whether you let others use your pendulum. I mean we are all channeling the same light. Some healers are very precious about sharing their tools. I have never felt the same way. Maybe I have always been surrounded by like-minded souls, so there was no reason. However, if you want to keep your pendulum only for yourself, stand firm, for we always know what way is best for us. Remember that everyone is different.

Asking for guidance when using pendulums

Although we can use the pendulum for guidance, I must admit that I find this area tricky. Over the years, I have discovered it is easy to get a wrong answer using a pendulum. I ask, but in my opinion, it is not always as good as direct guidance. You need to have extremely clear focus to be able to rely solely on the pendulum. Frequently, I have discovered that my own emotions and desires can get in the way. If I am feeling emotional or worried, I can directly alter the swing to get the outcome I want. If I already have my own block around the subject, it is even worse.

For example, asking about visiting the dentist is fraught with danger for some people. So when they ask whether they need to go, their own emotional response can alter the swing of the pendulum. Any highly-charged emotional question suffers in the same way. It is like our emotions and thoughts override the true answer. Be aware of this trap.

I love using it in healing and clearing. I use it less for other areas, preferring to ask Spirit to tell me directly. I never rely on it for yes or no answers. I use it to confirm a message or receive another angle.

Everyone has his or her own way to channel. You can read lots of books making suggestions and occasionally regulations. Ultimately, we all need to follow our own hearts and minds, as most of us have experienced a variety of psychic lives that we can draw from. The diversity of these lives means our skills and experiences will be varied.

Trust in your own intuition, for it lights your way to Spirit.

Life force of a person or animal

The pendulum can be used to show us the life force of a person or animal. When we are sending healing light to them, it can be useful to know how much life force they already have. Healthy, young people have large amounts of energy in their field. However, as we sicken or age this force becomes depleted. If the pendulum shows hardly any movement, this can be a sign that the person or animal may be crossing over soon. That does not necessarily mean that it is imminent, it may be months or years. It is like they leave the earth energetically before they leave physically.

I have found that a healthy life force appears as a big, robust swing of the pendulum, whereas a weak, small circle may indicate our time on earth is ending. Our life force has everything to do with our vitality and general wellbeing. When my Golden Retriever was ill, I could see his life force depleting. The day before he became very ill he only displayed a tiny circle when I checked him with the pendulum. It had lessened greatly overnight, and I knew he was going. He was already departing energetically from his physical body.

This depletion happens before the silver cord separates, and we finally depart. Keep in mind that when we leave, the energy leaves first. By checking someone's life force using the pendulum we can know where he or she is. If it is their time to go home, the healing light cannot hold them here. Even though we can be sending healing light, the life force can continue to lessen. Fortunately, the healing energy travels with them to the other side and assists them there for nothing is wasted.

Life force of food

Like all living things, foods have their own life force. You can check how much energy is in all foods by putting the pendulum on them. I just hold the pendulum over the food and watch how big the circle swings. It is fascinating to measure the amount in various foods. Of course, fresh fruit, vegetables, seeds and nuts all show a large, circular movement. However, the energetically dead foods like meats, some bread and most processed foods show little. Microwaved foods will all have a diminished life force.

You can check how much life is in the meals you eat. All you have to do is to place the pendulum above and wait to observe the swing. Checking with the pendulum helped me to "see" the life force in the foods that I was eating. Then in an effort to nourish myself, I could make better, more informed choices. It can help you as well.

If you keep an apple or orange for a few weeks, you can track the diminishing energy flow. These days it can be difficult to know how fresh our food is, but with one check of the pendulum, you will know. I discovered when food was not good to eat the pendulum went backwards. Really freaky!

Having an extra set of eyes energetically is so valuable. Have fun and check some of your herbs and medicines. In my experiment, I noticed that the essences and oils showed huge amounts of energy. Even some water contained noticeable energy. Several months ago I used a mustard pack on my foot to release some toxins. Before I used the mustard plaster, I checked its energy. It was big and flowing with the pendulum showing a healthy swing. After removing the plaster, I checked it again and was astounded. The pendulum was going around just as big, but in the reverse. I was seeing the amount of released energy the mustard pack had absorbed. It was great to be able to see the way the plaster had worked.

The pendulum definitely can be used to show us energy. Experiment and find out your own truths.

Using your body as a pendulum

Your body can be used as a pendulum. I discovered this when I was researching kinesiology where one of the methods used was asking the body directly. To do this you stand upright with your feet planted firmly on the ground. Next, decide what way you wish to use your body. I programmed a forward swaying of my body as a positive and a backward movement indicating a negative. Then I held my hands to my heart chakra and asked my body a question. I focused very intently, and waited for my body to reply by swaying backwards or forwards. This new method took a bit of time to master, but seemed very good.

After several attempts, it dawned on me why it worked. This method was using my body like an energetic pendulum. Our body has an energy, which connects into universal energy. I was so excited, and began experimenting by asking my "pendulum" body various questions. Then I double-checked with the other kinesiology techniques. All concurred.

In addition, you use it to ask whether your body likes certain foods and medicines. All you do is to hold the item to your heart and ask if it is good for your aura. By observing how the body sways you can make healthy choices.

Using your own body as a pendulum is a splendid way to tap into your own knowing. Our aura speaks to us all the time. We just have to learn how to hear it. With this method, we can access much information, and, with practice and focus, come to know ourselves better.

How the Aura Works

All is noted in the spiritual library above. Even the smallest gesture of love shines brightly in your book of life.

The layers of the aura

Scores of books have been written about the aural layers and what they signify. Many people consider that there are seven layers, while some, like me, believe there is only one layer, which varies in energetic vibration.

It has been written that the first layer, which is the densest one energetically, is called the Etheric Body/Layer. This energy layer underpins all the actual physical organs and structures in the body. If we could see the etheric part, it would look like a light image of the body. In the first layer resides the dense physical body together with the etheric part. The Etheric Body/Layer passes through the body and extends out a few centimeters all around it. This layer connects with the first chakra and involves our organs, the glands and the acupuncture system. Basically, the first layer concerns the health of our physical body.

The second layer is named the Emotional Body/Layer, and it lies about five centimeters from the physical body. This layer is in constant motion as it processes our feelings like fear, anger and grief. It corresponds to the second chakra. The emotions in the second layer can filter through to the first layer and can affect the physical body. These feelings can present as headaches, digestive problems, skin rashes, etc.

The Mental Body/Layer is the third layer, and it is where we store our thoughts, ideas, and patterns of thinking. People hold knowledge and belief systems here. Unfortunately, it is also where rigid ideas and prejudices can be held. This layer connects to the third chakra, and some people think it radiates a yellow light. If there are mental health issues, they may be found in this place.

The Astral Body/Layer is the fourth body and is a very important layer in terms of relationships and emotions. It sits further out from the physical body and is rose-colored, like love. The Astral Layer/Body is the interface between the first three layers and the last three layers, which are more concerned with our spiritual side. Many blocks reside in the astral body, and they commonly revolve around unresolved traumas.

The Etheric Template Body/Layer is the fifth layer, and this is a copy of the physical body on the spiritual plane. This is where our higher consciousness and will reside. Creativity and communication are important elements of this layer, which connects to the throat chakra.

The Celestial Body/Layer is where we move to the spiritual world through meditation, prayers, etc. and come to experience life as more than just human. Our spiritual side is reflected in the connection to the sixth chakra, which is the third eye. Some people think this layer is connected to the subconscious.

The outermost layer may extend a meter or more from the physical body and is called the Causal or Ketheric Template Layer/Body. With its connection to the crown chakra, it joins into the universal mind and our experience of our God. This last layer protects and holds the aura together. Some think it contains the copy of all of our soul lives.

Although I have explained how others view the seven layers, I must admit to being guided to another belief. In the above, I have written that the layers or bodies seem to be individual layers from one to seven. However, I think the layers are like veils one on top of the other, where each veil is vibrating at its own frequency. It seems to me that the layers are all the same energy, the same light. I know that my thoughts go against much that has been written. The seven layers template has been formed and supported by numerous spiritual people. In spite of this, I understand the template is only a guide, and is not the only truth. My view of the layers is not like others; however, you must decide for yourself.

In addition, I don't feel the layers are a predestined distance apart, but vary from person to person. Individuals will design their own aura according to their own needs. Our auras are varying sizes, similar to our physical differences. Therefore, our aural layers could also vary.

We all come in with our unique blueprint, with no one following the exact formula set out by other people's beliefs.

The importance of the layers is in understanding how the light supports us. Energetically, we are layers of varying vibrational energy, and this light is our fundamental life force through time and space.

It is who we are and all there is. As we are one, so we are the Oneness of all, the Light.

Storing energies throughout the layers

We all store our experiences throughout the aura, and so we have vibrating layers interspersed with our own personal collection of energies. For the most part, people are totally unaware of these energies swirling in their aura. These energies are bundles of light containing all our present and past-life experiences, and as such they bring with them many life lessons and gifts. This abundance of knowledge can be activated in each new life. Personally, I feel that these energies within our auras can be a positive force enabling us to do much soul growth. In these aural energies, there are unresolved lessons and experiences that the soul may wish to work on in this life. Fears and phobias, likes and dislikes and personal difficulties in relationships can be carried through from life to life.

We come in with plans of what we will try to address this time. It is in the Garden of Remembrance that we made these decisions. Frequently, challenges that we have not dealt with in other lives can come up to be resolved in this life, or gifts we did not choose to develop before can be used again. The earth life is the life of choice, for here we truly are the masters of our destiny. This world offers us a myriad of choices to work through our lessons and usually our only limitations are ourselves.

So, we are dealing with past-life and present-life issues. At times, it is easy to work out where the issues come from. It may be obvious that what we are working through is from the present, while other times it is from the past. As a rule, inexplicable dislikes are rooted in past lives. Perhaps we have had a bad experience with that place, food or person in some other life. It will have no connection with this life. Part of personal growth is finding ways to work through our issues. It is then that they can be felt and released, even if they originated from the past.

Emotions are commonly stored throughout the aura. There can be several emotions carried even within one layer. Hate, fear, sadness, etc. can all exist on one layer. People who struggle with letting things go may become burdened with these emotions. The more feelings carried through the layers, the heavier and more clogged up the aura becomes.

Everyone comes in vibrating at his or her own rate. Spiritually evolved souls come in vibrating high. However, if they allow the energies to build up and don't release them, gradually their aura's rate slows down.

To evolve spiritually and be healthy, we need to be vibrating at the best rate for our body. By letting go of old emotions, we can lighten our load and quicken the vibration of the aura. If we want to grow spiritually, release work will help to speed up the process.

We may vibrate at various rates, radiate different colors and be filled with diverse thoughts, but essentially we are the same at the core, for we all carry the same light. It is the energies that separate us and make us seem dissimilar.

The Light we bring from the other side shines brightly and is the spark in all of us. It is our common core, the essence of life.

The acupuncture channels and nadis

The acupuncture channels are the interface between the physical body and the chakras. There are many meridians running through the body feeding the aura and maintaining a vigorous energy flow. The correct flow is very important for overall health, as blockages can cause illness. Centuries ago, there was an enlightened person who had the ability to see the lines of light whizzing through the meridians, and he recorded where they were located. Nowadays, a trained acupuncturist will know where the points are. All the meridians are looped together and run like a huge track throughout the body. So, if one meridian is over-energized or under-energized, it will directly affect the running of all the channels. To correct the flow, the acupuncturist will seek to rectify the balance.

If we study where the important acupuncture points are around the body, we can work on them. By pressing or massaging these points we can shift the energy, and even sense this energy moving around our body.

Another way to help clear our channels is to work on our hands and feet because most of the channels begin and end in these areas. To give ourselves healing, we only have to work on the fingers and toes, for by holding each digit for a while we can channel in energy and support the meridians. Any energy we can send through our hands will feed all the meridians and can assist in balancing our entire field. I hold my fingers or toes one by one with my hand. Many times I can feel throbbing energy and tingling in my fingers and toes when I do this. Sometimes, I have felt pain. There are occasions when holding my fingers or toes that I have felt the energy moving through to other parts of my body. On these occasions, I keep holding the particular finger or toe until it seems the energy has stopped moving.

The nadi system is another energy system, however it is unlike acupuncture. With the acupuncture points, we can actually locate them on the physical body, while the nadis are inaccessible in our physical space. In terms of yogic understanding, there are about seventy-two thousand nadis running through the astral body, and it is through these tubes or nerve channels that the energy flows. There are three significant channels. The main nadi, called the Sushumna, runs up the back where our spine is. The Kundalini lies at the base of the spine, and it is here that the energy lies resembling a coiled snake. Yogic practices can activate the Kundalini and release this energy. When the Kundalini energy rises up the spine and reaches the crown, the yogis believe we have reached Samadhi, which is the state of being in the super consciousness. On each side of the main nadi lie the Ida and Pingala. These major nadis intertwine up the body. Yoga practices are designed to clear and purify these channels by moving the energy. Many believe that by doing yoga that the nadis can be affected positively and blockages released. Therefore, yoga is seen as an energy medicine for the entire system.

The chakras

Apart from the physical body, the acupuncture points and nadis we also have the chakras. The chakras, the meridians and nadis work independently, but do influence each other. All energy goes to where it is needed most, so by working on one system, the others will benefit.

Chakras are spinning vortices of light, and we have several major ones in the front and back of the body. The main chakras lie on the front of the head and torso and behind our head and down the spine. There are smaller chakras throughout the aura.

Each chakra has four major aspects, namely, the physical, emotional, mental and spiritual. Physical injuries happen to the body, so if we hurt our hand by knocking it, that would manifest in the physical part of the chakra. The emotions of grief, fear and anger, etc. can upset the fine balance of the chakras. In healing work we call these blocks. Mental issues can disturb the chakra, as the way that we think can constrict our energy flow.

The spiritual aspect concerns our past lives and karmic lessons. Information is stored in the chakras, and when we embrace the learning surrounding our past lives, these chakras can eventually be cleared. If we are on the spiritual path, our chakras can become more open and vibrate at a higher rate, thereby advantaging our spiritual journey, as well as our health. Our ability to channel, do healing work or pick up our personal power is heightened once these chakras are cleared.

The base chakra, also known as the root chakra, sits between our legs. If we could see the base chakra, it would look like a spinning, red vortex. This chakra spins at the slowest rate of all the chakras and has an earthy quality to it. If our base is balanced, we feel grounded and at one with the world. The base feeds the area it resides in and the flow of energy to the legs and feet. It governs our place in the world and our sense of survival. I believe we can hold much anger and fear in this chakra.

The sacral chakra sits above the base chakra and below the navel; it is bright orange and vibrates a little higher than the base chakra. Our sexuality is expressed here, and emotionally it is our pleasure and joy centre. Like the base, much fear and anger can be held in this chakra.

I like to include the navel area, even though it may be overlooked by some teachings. In my opinion, it is our most developed chakra. From our moment of conception, it becomes our lifeline. The navel chakra is a giant receiver, and it is the first point of connection once on earth. This chakra has a dual purpose; one is connected to our survival, and the other is of a spiritual nature. The umbilical cord is connected to our physical mother, disconnecting once we are born. When the physical cord is cut, we become an individual and part of the universal earth energy.

Another very important aspect of the navel chakra is its spiritual nature. Before we arrived it was our connection point to the spiritual realm, and this continues once the physical cord is severed. I believe that when we die, our energetic umbilical cord remains intact for the journey back to Spirit. Much pain can be held in this chakra. If you put your hands over this point, you can regularly feel it releasing. I always include the navel chakra in my healing, as I have found much unexpressed emotion is trapped here. In many ways, I feel it is the storehouse of all we are.

The solar plexus chakra is our stomach area and governs our digestion. This chakra is bright yellow. Many people feel most of their emotions in the solar plexus, and it is here we try to digest our world. Remember, not only food is digested in the solar plexus. Digestion occurs on many levels, physically, emotionally and mentally. If we are working through digesting difficult emotions or mental thoughts, this chakra is directly affected. Our personal power sits in this chakra, and a good energy flow helps us stand in our own power. However, a weakened flow can make us feel powerless and out of control.

The heart chakra is located at the middle of the chest. Some people believe it resonates with the color green, while others believe it to be pink. The heart chakra is where much healing and love can be sent. Many people use the heart chakra to channel in healing light. Therefore, the more open this chakra, the more light we will be able to channel. It is here that major blocks can manifest as the heart chakra comes under much attack in relationships. Emotional hurts, like loss and grief, can cripple this area, so to avoid this we put up shields as protection. Unfortunately, these shields can affect the flow to the heart area and alter the spin of the chakra.

Everyone has met people who, once hurt, never let down the shield and continue to live unhappy lives. If only they could release their shields, love could be in their world again. In time, some recover and come out to love; however, many hide behind their barrier. These energetic blocks restrict the flow to the heart and can eventually cause problems around the chest.

On the left between the heart chakra and solar plexus chakra sits the splenic chakra. There is a reference to the splenic chakra in eastern writings. It is situated in the middle part of the left bottom rib and like the other major chakras, it has a back counterpart. The significance of the splenic chakra is that it is a major point of entry for energy. When energy, and especially air energy enters, it is sent to all the other chakras. The splenic chakra oversees our immune system and aids digestion. The term "venting your spleen" indicates when we are holding much unexpressed anger in this area. Many children use this chakra to hide the anger they can feel towards their parents or authority figures.

The throat chakra is at the base of the neck and vibrates in the blue spectrum. Creative ideas and abilities are found in this chakra, and if you want to evolve in these areas work on opening up your throat chakra. Speaking your truth helps to keep your throat chakra clear. Most throat problems come from bottled-up feelings of anger and grief. The effect of this can make us controlling and needy at the same time.

The brow chakra or third eye is positioned between the eyebrows. The color is indigo. The third eye acts as our intuitive eye, as we can see what the human eye does not see. The third eye is an extremely powerful chakra. Fully developed and during meditation, it can open us up to the spiritual world in amazing ways. There are advanced beings who can feel the chakra spinning and whirling whenever they meditate, channel or do healing work. If you watch a person who is channeling you can literally see the area around the third eye moving.

On the forehead, there is another lesser-known chakra. It sits just above the third eye where the hairline starts. I believe, as we advance, this chakra will begin to spin larger, and we will become more aware of its presence. At this point, it is just beginning to activate. Given time, it will develop, and we can progress further on our spiritual journey.

On the top of the head sits the crown chakra. White light usually streams into a healthy crown, and this helps us to connect with the universal light and the higher energies. A strong connection to Spirit is easier when the crown is fully open. However, when it is closed, we will find it hard to meditate effectively or channel clearly. We can suffer from depression and sleep disorders when this chakra is spinning incorrectly. The crown chakra vibrates at the highest rate of all the chakras. I always feel the crown chakra is like the icing on the cake.

The chakras on the front of our body have their counterparts on the back. As a result, if we looked at ourselves from the side, there will be the back and front chakras. The other important chakras are on the hands, feet, knees, hips and shoulders. The entire aura is covered by many other chakras.

In addition, some teachings include chakras between the knees, the feet and two higher-level ones above the crown. Little is known about these higher chakras but in the years to come all will be revealed.

Minor chakras

Each major chakra has two companion chakras to help support it. They are like the backup system for the main one, and these smaller chakras keep the left and right of the body aligned. When necessary the smaller chakras supply and help to balance the major chakras. They store excess energy to be used in times of depletion and release energy when needed.

Physical, emotional, mental and spiritual issues affect these chakras. They might be smaller, but they remain significant energy sources.

The minor base chakras feed the left and right leg, while the minor sacral chakras serve the ovaries/testes and hip areas. The naval chakras assist the left and right side of the bowel. The solar plexus chakra has different organs operating on each side with the smaller right chakra serving the liver and gallbladder, while the minor left chakra feeds the stomach and spleen. The minor heart chakras serve the heart and each respective lung, right and left. The throat supports the left and right side of the thyroid and parathyroid glands. Both eyes and ears are helped by the third-eye minor chakras, and they also assist with the brain. And last, but not least, the crown chakras support the left and right sides of the brain.

Like the main chakras, these smaller chakras can be damaged and spin incorrectly and so any dysfunction will affect the major chakra.

Any healing work done on the major chakras will flow into the little ones. Sometimes, I have done healings where the focus was on fixing these minor chakras. When I work, I never focus only on the main chakras, but let the healing be guided to these chakras when necessary.

When I was recovering from my illness, I went to a healer for energy work. She talked about the fact that my seven minor heart chakras were in need of some help. These seven little chakras run up from the bottom of our breastbone to the top. In my understanding, they serve to support the heart chakra and spiritually enable us to open up more to Spirit. You may find it an interesting meditation to ask that your own small heart chakras be healed and opened. In addition, you could work on them with a pendulum or massage these points. I feel that once we know about certain new centers around the body that we can easily include them in our healing sessions. It is said that knowledge is power.

In my experience, there are minor chakras on the ears, eyes, cheek sinus areas, the liver, the stomach, ovaries, elbows, middle of the back of calves, the ankles, middle of each buttock, kidneys, the thymus, temples, the breasts, etc. If you use a pendulum you can locate and work on these places. The body is covered with numerous chakras, similar to the countless acupuncture points. When you work, be open to exploring all the different chakras and don't be held by rigid ideas of where they are. Each person is energetically unique with their own individual pattern. Therefore, be willing to work all over the body using your own intuition.

As we progress, I believe more and more chakras will emerge as part of our knowledge base. The world is opening up on so many levels, just like our auras.

Seven eyes and chakra connection

Physically, we have the right and left eye. However, spiritually we have seven eyes, including the two physical eyes. Apart from the physical eyes, there are five other spiritual eyes sitting on the forehead in a line from where the eyebrows meet, to just behind the hairline. They lie on a major acupuncture meridian called the Du or Governing Vessel.

These seven eyes actually correspond to each major chakra. This piece of information is a new way of viewing the connection between the seven eyes and the seven major chakras.

The base chakra is reflected in the right eye, while the left eye corresponds to the sacral chakra. The first two eyes deal directly with the more physical aspects of the world. Sight helps us to exist on earth because it enables us to see what is really occurring. As we all know, we can learn much about a person by observing them.

The third eye corresponds to the solar plexus. This eye is a finer gauge of a similar process used by our physical eyes. By viewing with the third eye we feel and see the way the situation is truly playing out. The solar plexus is our emotion centre and like the third eye, it is our trust barometer. We digest what is presented and work out how we feel about it and if something does not ring true, we sense it. An open third eye means we can access spiritual guidance.

The fourth eye is the heart chakra and is our connection to God and the love energy. With an open heart chakra, there is every chance our fourth eye is functioning on some level.

The fifth eye is our throat chakra. It deals with the communication with Spirit. Just as we use the throat to speak to others, so we use the fifth eye to speak to Spirit. With an open fifth eye we can become a channel for Spirit, and past lives can be read from this eye too.

The sixth is a finer more highly tuned third eye. We can receive heightened information when this eye is open. I believe some can see Spirit when this eye is active.

The seventh eye is our direct connection to the universe. Like the crown, it can transcend all there is and all there is to come. An open seventh eye relates directly to our relationship with God.

Few people have all seven eyes fully opened, and I think the average person seems to have only the first three open. However, we can ask for these seven eyes to be opened to enable us spiritually to ascend more easily. Just remember, due to our spiritual journey, we may only be able to access information using these eyes when the time is right. All in divine timing.

The seven eye lens

While meditating, I was shown how the seven eyes can actually be energetically joined up to make an energetic lens.

To begin with, imagine a line of energy going horizontally from the right eye to the left. Then make the two sides of the triangle by energetically sending light in a straight line from each eye to the third eye. This will make the first triangle.

The next line is from the right eye to the left again, but this time the two lines from the eyes connect to the fourth eye. We keep repeating this process with each eye until we reach the seventh eye.

When these lines join up a unique energy structure is formed, and our third eye becomes amazingly powerful. Each of the triangular shapes acts as a compounding lens to heighten focus of the third eye, like a microscope. By doing this work several times, the third eye becomes a more concentrated source of light, and all psychic work will be advantaged.

Once I worked out how to make the energy lens, it became easy to do whenever I wished to enhance my intuitive gift. I believe everyone can benefit from energetically enhancing his or her third eye in this manner. I found this new way to heighten our spiritual journey was a fascinating discovery.

Chakra energy cores and the glands

I think that inside every chakra there resides a concentrated core of energy. To me, it looks like a ball of light shining right in the centre of the chakra. It is important that this energetic core is sound, for without a sturdy core the chakra will have a wobbly base. This core energy is very interesting. The energy seems to be a more condensed form than in the rest of the aura. These cores of light lie deep within the actual physical body and this core energy is the engine of each chakra.

The cores all vibrate at the same rate, and within each core is contained the frequencies and colors of every individual chakra. It is only when the chakras begin to spin out into the aura that they take on their own vibrational rate. Once they begin to spin out into the energy field each chakra then spins into its own color. The deep light inside each core is the same light from the same essence; it all comes from the higher Source. This core light has a huge impact upon us. It is the very essence of life and the connection to all there is. It is the Oneness, the Light.

I have felt this core light. You may have as well. After my accident, I felt that the light in my chakras was flickering and weak. I could sense the lights were not burning brightly like before. The importance of this core energy is enormous, for when these lights go out it can mean the end of our life on earth.

Strong core energy in every chakra signifies energetic strength. I believe our chakras are only as robust as their individual core base. I think the light cores are our spiritual bodies, our soul lights. I suspect that with human sight, we are unable to "see" the cores, as it is a light unperceivable to our eyes.

The chakra cores are closely connected to the endocrine glands. These glands physically feed the body, and in turn the glands are fed by the core energies. The glands are mini-versions of the inner cores and have their own core energy from which they run. This is independent of the chakra cores. The endocrine glands correspond to the chakras. As yet modern medicine has not understood the importance of these glands. Of course, they are physical functioning parts of the body, but beyond that they are another complex energetic nervous system. Each has its own function, but in synchrony, they form an energy machine that runs the body.

The vibration of each gland is extremely important. They underpin the chakra system and as such their vibrational rate is different, but they are also synchronized, each one feeding the other.

Activating these glands will dramatically affect our wellbeing. The glands I focus on are the adrenals, the ovaries or testes, the pancreas, the thymus, the thyroid, the pineal and the pituitary. You can actually work on each gland by using thought. To do so, I begin by focusing on each gland, and then I mentally increase the vibration to the correct vibrational rate. You don't need to know the rate because it is your intention that will increase the vibration to the right rate. Remember, our mind can perform incredible energy balancing. Once I feel I have reached the right rate, I fill each gland with healing light. You can focus on the colors of the individual chakras if you wish.

In some cultures, shamans learnt how to vibrate their pineal gland. As a test they were put into a dark cave and couldn't leave until they could produce light from the pineal. There is a special light quality connected to the pineal which can be used to manifest light, a psychic light.

I have felt the light flash when I have vibrated my third eye. I am not saying I did what the shaman did. I think it just shows that the pineal is a concentrated source of light.

I can feel my third-eye chakra spinning during some meditations and hear it whirring in my aura. There is sometimes a light flash, but not always. You may have experienced a big light flash when meditating. It is the pineal gland activating. The light coming in from the universe is being read by the gland, and in these situations, the pineal can feel like it is vibrating inside of your head. It's a wild experience. So when you begin to work on yourself, don't be surprised if you have similar outcomes.

I believe our body is always singing its own tune. Some skilled healers can psychically hear the sound of the aura. To these "sensitives" the body really sings. As part of the healing, these people will sing or make sounds into the chakras to bring the glands into "tune." This practice is called toning.

The various chakras have their individual vibration, but they all sing together. One is reliant on the other for the song; some notes higher and some lower, but always in the same key.

Chakra conduits

The chakras are all connected to each other. There is a line of energy running from the base chakra to the sacral, the sacral to the solar plexus and so on. These connecting links are very important to the flow of the aura. I have read much about the chakras, but little about these connecting energy channels. The chakras "talk" to each other energetically via these connections.

Two problems can occur if a chakra is damaged. The flow of the energy will be hindered and/or the conduit can be blocking the flow. These disconnections can separate the aura into segments. Often, people can sense when the energy in their aura is not flowing properly. They can feel something is wrong, but can't quite work out what is it. Many describe the feelings as being disconnected, emotionally or mentally. I have found that conduit blocks between the chakras seriously affect us. When I do healing work, I consciously ask that the light be moved through the conduits, not only into the chakras. In Reiki, the two hands are normally working on two chakras, which then help to shift energy in the conduits.

Interestingly, these conduits exist in acupuncture charts. Two major channels run up the front and back of the body, the Conception Vessel in the front and the Governor at the back. There are over twenty acupuncture points on each channel.

However, there is little mention of the importance of the conduits in healing work. Being aware of their significance and consciously working on them will enhance your healing outcomes.

Chakra damage

The best aura to have is the one where all the chakras are spinning in the correct direction, equally balanced and the layers correctly aligned. Mostly, we all come into the world balanced and full of light. Even so, for some of us, the aura does not remain the same, as life in general takes its toll.

Chakras can be damaged in many ways. They can be over-energized or under-energized, torn or off balance and some can have gaping holes in them. Once a chakra becomes damaged, it will not be long before physical problems manifest. If the person has put up a block anywhere around the body, the flow of energy around the chakra will be compromised. Eventually, it will affect the working of the chakra and put an additional strain on another chakra. After a while, the chakras can begin to spin either more slowly or too quickly. An under-functioning chakra can cease to supply energy to the chakra above and below. Sometimes, the actual channel between two chakras can be blocked.

They say a chakra is never closed completely, but any shutdown is not good. Without enough energy, the chakra cannot perform its duties to the full. Over time, the particular area becomes less efficient and cannot supply energy to the organs it is in charge of.

Our emotions are often the reason why our chakras start to malfunction. Chakras can lose balance when they are filled with fear, anger, grief or any other negative emotion. Shocks, frightening experiences, depression and despair can shut chakras down. Too much negativity will slow these energy channels, so dealing with and releasing bottled emotions can lighten the chakras and help them come back to full speed.

Serious illness is signaled by stagnation around the body. The energy is not flowing freely, and so our health is compromised. Without a good flow of energy, the body cannot perform its daily functions with a resultant lowering of the immune system.

The chakras spin from inside of the physical body out to the outer skin covering the aura. I believe we start closing down from the edge of the aura. This happens years before any major problem is found in the body. With less and less light coming in, the chakra's light gets dimmer and dimmer. That's why sick people look so sallow, because there is little light shining in their aura. Without healthy energy flow, the physical body begins to struggle and starts to break down. What has been happening for ages on the outside now manifests on the inside, in the physical body. Good health is totally dependent on a strong energy body with all the chakras working together to support life and wellbeing. Without this basic mechanism, we will become sick.

People frequently begin to live outside of their bodies when the physical body becomes compromised. Extreme examples of this happening are coma and dementia patients. They continue to exist, but not in the normal way. They are alive, but existing out of their bodies with a cord allowing them to come in and out. Just before death the same thing happens, but the cord weakens and eventually separates from the physical body.

Healers who specialize in working with energy can mend or balance the chakras. However, some people will reset their energy body following the work. This is because when we release negative energy from the body, it can bring up emotional or mental issues. If the person is unwilling to deal with these difficult issues, they reset their body. I have seen this happen many times. The mind is a powerful weapon, which can be used to stop change or embrace change.

Lifestyle changes, positive thinking and meditation can help realign the chakras. We can cleanse ourselves by seeing the various chakras releasing unwanted energy and being filled with light.

The aura can be balanced with good intentions and healing work. In my work as a healer, I have encountered several energy patterns that clients display. It is unusual to see someone with all chakras spinning properly once they are in their thirties. In the cases where they are all spinning, I have found the person to be already tackling their issues, deeply involved in meditation or spiritual work and/or having experienced a particularly stress-free life.

A person experiencing physical or emotional problems will normally have one or more dysfunctional chakras around the related area. Anyone who has been subjected to abuse may have the lower three chakras closed down. These individuals adapt by manifesting all of their energy from the top part of their bodies. This lack of flow from the stomach down creates problems and sooner or later, their health becomes compromised. Without adequate energy running through all the major chakras, the person suffers from fatigue. They work on half-strength, as the energy running in the lower half of their body is so much less. It's like having a garden that's only half-watered.

Anyone with emotional issues regularly has an under-functioning heart chakra. Given time problems will manifest in the chest area and affect the nerves. Depression affects the crown and there will be little energy flowing. People will find it hard to connect on a spiritual level when the crown is not open. If someone has lived in a frightening situation, the base chakra spins poorly. This directly affects the stability and general strength of the person. Power imbalances show up in the solar plexus. Either the person has a very inadequate spin and displays little personal power, or as a reaction to their situation, has an overly big solar plexus in order to gain the power back.

Repeatedly, wherever there is a problem in the physical body, we will find the chakra around that area to be unbalanced and not functioning correctly.

The best pattern to have is when all the chakras are spinning correctly. The chakras take in energy from the universal light. They "breathe" it in and then out. If a chakra can't "breathe" energetically, the whole aura will be weakened.

Leaks, holes and misalignment in the aura

As mentioned before, the aura resembles a bubble with our personal energy being contained in the bubble, which is similar to our skin. The edge of the aura vibrates extremely fast. Its quality is elastic and durable, and the bubble coating has an extra thickness of energy for added protection.

However, even with protection, the aural skin can be torn or damaged. The more damage the outside layer sustains, the worse it is for our future health. Traumas to the aura can start the holes, and once damaged the holes can get bigger. The tears and holes arise from different experiences. We can get them in accidents or from traumatic episodes. They can come from physical, emotional and mental damage.

The most obvious one is physical damage from daily life. We injure the aura by damaging the body. Whenever we injure the physical body, the energy body is also injured. For example, if we were in a car accident or having surgery, both the physical and energy bodies would be cut.

Emotional cuts are no different. For example, we may feel "stabbed" by someone we love and this would create a hole. Hurts of the heart show up as holes in the aura. Everyone has felt an energetic knife attack. Occasionally, these emotional knife wounds are large. With some people, there are many smaller knives in various positions, and these gaping wounds eventually cause the leaking of energy.

Mental abuse can penetrate our fine bubble. The constant attack weakens the coating, and breaks appear. These attacks can persist until the person can no longer maintain their protective eggshell coating. The harsh words and constant assaults form a stretched part and like plastic wrap the pressure makes it thinner, and finally, it breaks. Mostly, this type of damage is unrecognized. A nagging parent, a dominating partner or child, a demanding boss or power-hungry friend can create these holes.

In addition, we can be responsible for making holes ourselves. The soul always protects itself, and we know how to get out of our body before any terrifying or life-threatening event occurs. If it seems the physical body is about to be in danger the soul moves out of the aura. The exit is automatic and swift. In a sense, time stands still. The protection of the soul is paramount, for, unlike the human body which dies the soul remains. It has to last through eternity, and so we will do whatever is necessary to keep our soul intact. All of us know how to exit from our bodies. Exiting suddenly every now and then is all right as the aura can realign itself. Sometimes, we exit when we sleep, in meditation, and when we astral travel. However, when we leave the body in these situations, the method is gradual and gentle, like floating off and then coming back in.

The way we exit is important. Trauma makes us burst out of the aura, very suddenly and without care, which over time, can form large exit holes. Years of abuse and trauma are common situations where holes and tears can occur. Victims of abuse suffer in this way, as do soldiers and victims of violent crimes. Those who have to endure these episodes learn how to escape from their body. After repeated trauma, holes can form around the exit points, with these points becoming permanent holes in the aura. Unfortunately, some need to exit over and over again. As soon as they sense danger they are out. Children living in abusive homes learn how to do this at a very young age. After a couple of terrifying episodes, they are skilled at the escape and learn how to live outside of their aura until it is safe to return.

Unfortunately, in the rush we don't always get back into our energy bodies properly. Jumping out can create a problem for getting back because, in returning, we can leave bits of our energy behind out there. Parts can be left out with the universal energy which is like leaving a bit of the soul outside of the aura.

There is another problem. As we try to get back in we can overlap the energy body. Maybe we don't quite get back in properly. The saying that "You are beside yourself" can be technically true. This misalignment is common. I believe post-traumatic stress is a result of these misalignments. The aura functions as a balanced unit, therefore, when one bit is not completely aligned or missing, it alters the whole.

Extreme pain can make us leave the body quickly, that is why people pass out. Sadly, this option is not good as the exit hole allows leakage, and so our health is compromised. As a consequence physical problems, mental issues and emotional instability can result.

Lastly, some poor souls get lost out there and may not have enough energy to get back in. Dementia patients regularly float around out of their bodies. Sadly, they weaken energetically, finding it too hard to get back in again. They just don't have enough energy, and eventually they live out there. Understanding the mechanics of misalignment can explain many phenomena. We can live outside for a while, but it is best to live in your aura if you wish to stay healthy.

Don't worry if you think you have experienced the above. A good healer can mend the holes, stop the leaks and realign the aura by filling the holes and sealing them with light.

I believe we can realign our energy body using our own mind. Think of the vibrating layer I mentioned earlier sitting in the aura, like those Russian dolls one sitting inside the other. Next, visualize them as light. In that way, the first inner body shines through to the edge of the body. The first body is the physical one. It is made of flesh and bone; however, it is also made of light.

Mentally line up all the other six bodies from the core to the edge of the aura. Bring the light in through your head and push it through the bodies. Fill them with the amount of light they need and cover the entire eggshell edge with gold light.

Physically, you can also work on yourself. You may have places around the aura corresponding to where you have physical problems. There are probably holes there. These are the places to begin. Start by holding your hands above or directly on your body. Do what feels comfortable. Send the light through your hands into the spot and imagine filling up the gap with light. Be patient, as it can take quite a long time to fill up some parts. While doing this work you can experience a strange sensation. Sometimes, when you hold your hands above your body, they can automatically move. What happens is that the light fills up the area, and your hands will move further out to the next section of the aura. I found the hand moves almost of its own accord, frequently with a clunking feeling. It is pretty amazing.

The body is a self-healing machine. All it does is try to heal itself, so remember that we can assist it with intention and good healing methods.

The Beauty of the Healing Lights

Fill and surround yourself with color for it will alter your aura in ways beyond your comprehension.

Various light frequencies

Just as there are different colors in the world, so there are different light frequencies. These lights come from our universe, and also from unknown dimensions and galaxies.

Over the years, I have learnt how to work with some of these incredible light energies. They not only hold the universal light, but also include other qualities as yet unrecognized here on earth. Light is not only made of colors; it contains many other components.

Once we begin to work with these lights, we can draw other energies into our aura. In my opinion, emotions like love and joy can be held in particular lights. The more we work with these lights, the higher can be our personal ascension and connection to the spiritual world.

Love light

Most of mankind's woes stem from a lack of love. Love is all around us, just like the song says, but most of us lack it in our auras. It is as if we have forgotten how to be in love. I don't mean with another person. I mean to be in a state of love energetically.

Love is an actual energy, and it can be found in the light. We can access the love light. When I have used it, I saw it as pure energy composed of exquisitely colored lights dancing and swirling around each other; it's a spiral of radiant, ever-changing hues. Love light has warmth, a glow of beauty unseen by the human eye. Love exists in the spiritual world, as well as our physical one.

Love light is limitless and eternal and, in itself, it transcends all there is. Love supports and nourishes the soul, and it is our most significant connection to the God Light. To bring this energy into our aura is very easy because we don't have to love anyone or anything to be filled with the love energy. All we have to do is consciously call in the love light. I ask the angels to assist me. It matters little whether we bring it in through the crown chakra or absorb it into the aura in our own way. The only requirement is being open to receiving love into our being, for the more we can absorb, the greater the healing of the soul. Besides, the more love in our aura, the higher we are able to vibrate.

Love energy can be sent to others and the world in general. We all send love in a social sense. During phone calls, and in sending cards, we express our love for others; for the most part, it is done without really thinking about our deeper intention. This understanding about the love light brings with it a power because once we understand that love is an energy that can be sent, its strength increases. It is in the act of consciously understanding that love is energy, a light, that we give it more validity.

Like an archer, we can project love to wherever we choose, just like Cupid. When I write about sending the love light, I mean in a soul sense. This process cannot be used to make someone love you. It is not a human love, as it transcends our interpretation of love. This universal love is greater than our human heart and mind can comprehend, a love with no conditions and no limits.

Once we begin to work with the love light everything will alter. By bringing it into our being our entire energy body will change. In sending it, our recipients are given a chance to be replenished and emotionally whole again.

We spend our entire lives pursuing love, to love and to be loved. It is the human condition. Yet, it is there for the asking, there for the receiving. I encourage you to ask for the love light to flood your aura and heal your hurts, past and present.

Healing light

Basically, healing light is a form of energy medicine and like a bottle of medicine, healing light heads straight for the troubled place. It is very specific. Although it comes from, and is part of the universal light, it has a special quality. This light will act like a magnet homing into the most depleted area in our aura and begin its work.

In my experience, I have found healing light has a warm, soothing quality as it vibrates gently through the energy body, cleansing the sick spots. In a sense, healing light has its own consciousness and will go to the areas where it is most needed. Many times when I have worked on people, I have witnessed its wisdom. Occasionally, during the healing, I have noticed the light is not going to the sore foot or back, as I would have thought. Even though the person might have come for work due to some problem, I noticed that the healing light was being sent to another part of the aura.

Sometimes, only I would know this, but there have been times when the person knew that the light was going somewhere else as they could feel it there. These days I accept the healing light goes to the neediest place. I don't question its inherent wisdom.

Healing light assists movement of physical, emotional and mental blocks because it goes straight to the source of the problem. When we access this light issues may come up for us to look at, then once dealt with, the aura can heal. I ask for healing light to support my energy body.

We all strive to be whole, so by filling our aura with this light the rips and tears can be mended. I try not to dictate where the light goes. Of course, you can ask for light to be sent to your sore foot, but remember that there may be other more important places in need of work.

Our soul and our guardians know more than our human side. Just know that if your foot does not heal, it may be because another area in your aura is being restored. I believe that in asking to be made whole again, we open ourselves up to complete healing.

Asking for physical, emotional or mental healing light

We can call in healing light for the various areas in our aura, and by being specific can ensure the best light is being called upon. These are the physical, emotional and mental healing lights.

For example, you may have hurt yourself on a physical level, fallen and broken your wrist or burnt your hand. In these instances, I recommend you draw in the physical healing light into the area. The same method can be used for emotional healing. By calling in the emotional healing light the problem is fixed with the right light. All of us struggle with our feelings. Hurt, anger, sadness and fear are all energies that the emotional healing light can help you with.

Mental healing light works in the same way. Anguish and mental torment can be eased when sent this light. It can soothe a frazzled mind and calm anxiety.

In asking specifically for a particular light we work on two levels. On one level, we recognize where the problem originates. Mostly, it is very clear. If your friend has died, it is all emotional. Alternatively, if your workload is ridiculous, you are mentally overwhelmed.

However, at other times, the problem may not be so obvious to you. You may think your headache is from a sore neck, a physical problem, when it may not be. I remember coming into the kitchen one morning with a terrible headache. The first question my son had for me was enlightening. He asked me whom I was angry with. I was taken aback. However, on reflection, I quickly realized that the source of my headache was anger and could identify the person who had caused my anger. Keep in mind that what appears as one thing could be something else.

Be aware that it can also present in the reverse order. A physical problem can cause mental and emotional distress. Unexpected physical sickness can begin to erode into other parts of your life. If you can't perform normally, you can get depressed and cranky. We have heard all the jokes about menopausal women. Even so, on closer observation even though they are exhibiting non-physical problems like irritation and depression, the source is found in the physical changes. Once these ladies move out of the physical issues menopause brings up, the emotional and mental problems settle. Likewise, people suffering from back injuries may begin with a physical complaint, but later begin to experience depression and anger because of their physical malady. In these cases, it would be better to send healing for all three areas, physical, emotional and mental.

Healing light sent to a problem will go straight to the source. I recommend sending healing light with this agenda in mind. You can bring it into your own aura and also send it to others. Lots of healing light will strengthen and support any depleted system and will be used appropriately by the recipient aura. Any residual will be "saved" to be used in the fullness of time.

Light work is a wondrous journey. All you need to do is to listen to your inner guidance and follow your instincts.

Calming light

Using calming light is a wonderful way to support us during difficult times. I have used it when going through fearful, anxious days. This light vibrates slowly with a thick and almost marshmallow-like quality. Bringing it in steadies our nerves and as it infuses throughout the energy body, it softens and creates peace.

When in need, I simply ask for the calming light to come into my being and fill me up. It is extremely helpful before tests, public speaking and fearful situations. You can choose when and where you will use it. If you want it can be brought in days or weeks before the event.

After bringing in this light, I feel a lessening of the fear and anxiety, similar to a slowing down of the "nervous" areas. Calming light can be brought in while we sit at the traffic lights or stand in the line at the supermarket. Just imagine inhaling the calming light and see it filtering through you. During the time that I am bringing in the calming light, I ask for Spirit to help me. There have been occasions when I have asked them to keep delivering it whenever necessary. Calming light can be sent to others, to animals and troubled places around the globe.

The world needs more peace. We all need, as individuals, to feel the calm. For it is in the calmness that we feel that we shift the earth's aura too.

Joy light

Being full of joy is blissful. As little souls we come in brimming with love and joy and everything is wondrous and new. Unfortunately, time and general living can zap our joy until we hardly have any left. Some people do manage to remain joyful through thick and thin, while for others, it is only a vague memory.

Joy is a high vibrating light and like love, it contains lustrous colors. If I were to describe them, they are like the golden rays of the sun or the glowing sunsets, rich and warm. It is interesting that the color range coincides with our human sense of joy, the golden yellows. Within the golden colors flash the gem lights. The gem lights are actual crystals, in a light form, encrusted in the light waves. These gems help to carry the light and bring extra energy into our field.

Joy is carried in the light around us. All we have to do is absorb it into our energy body. In addition, when we bring in the joy light, our immune system is strengthened. When life is tough and sad, joy light is a wonderful medicine for the body. For with extra joy light in the aura, we are more able to endure these hardships. All we have to do is to have the intention to bring it in, see joy entering our aura and flooding us with its golden light.

Joy is the essence of the rapture we feel. The more joy we hold, the younger the body feels, for joy is not a heavy energy. With more joy in your being, your sense of daily happiness can be heightened. Happiness is not solely reliant on an external world, but can be felt in our internal world. Children have an abundance of this light. Their wonder and delight in the world rest on this light. Just like children, we need to have an adequate supply of this light to feel youthful.

The joy light can be accessed through the free happiness of life. It can be found in the smallest flower in the garden or the simple beauty of being wrapped in sunshine. So when we are in these happy situations, remember to absorb the joy light into every cell of our being.

Strengthening light

Strengthening light is extremely useful in difficult times. We all have times of unrelenting pressure in which our strength is tested. Illness, emotional pain and financial hardship are only a few examples of these trying experiences.

During these periods, I suggest that you call upon spiritual assistance and ask for the strengthening light to come in. I see it like silver steel reinforcing our entire aura with every part being given an extra layer of resilience. This light is weightless, but ever so strong. I have asked to receive this light whenever I need support. There are times in our lives when we have to keep going. I am not just referring to the physical state. Sometimes, we have come to a point of not coping anymore with everything becoming too much to bear. It is in these situations the strengthening light will support us. Although as humans we do have reserves, at times it does not feel like it. We can get so low that it is hard to imagine going on. In my experience, channeling in the strengthening light can take us through to the next level.

Bringing the light in is simple and healing; it can be brought in anywhere and anytime. The supply is endless and can be used for many situations. There is always help from above; we just need to know how to access it. I suggest you keep filling up when life gets tough, and don't worry about how often you may need to do so. Simply keep accessing this light until you feel better.

Strengthening light is extremely good in highly demanding situations. Use it for yourself and send it to those who need it. The saying, "God give me the strength" can be applied quite literally by accessing this light.

Recharging light

Everyone is familiar with the way a battery works. Therefore, when I was shown how to recharge my aura, I found it fascinating. All of us get run-down and feel we need a charge, and with this energy work, it is easy to do.

Firstly, I focus and visualize energy coming into my crown. Next, I see it pulsating down through my whole aura and through to my feet. Then I pulsate another charge of energy from my head to my feet again. I keep repeating the recharging until I feel it is time to stop. This recharge light is very helpful during tiring and stressful times. Not only does it refill the aura, but it also flushes out any fatiguing energy as it moves through from the crown to the feet.

I believe as we advance, we will know intuitively which light to use for every occasion. It was a new and exciting lesson for me to use this light in such a way. There is something almost hypnotic about the recharging process, and I believe it assists in relaxing us as well. This process can be used while waiting for an appointment or before an important meeting in which we need to feel fully energized. Of course, as with all energy work, it can be sent to others in similar need.

Have fun trying this one out and remember that all is provided for us, for Spirit gives all.

White light

Although I have already written about white light in "Spiritual Answers for Health and Happiness" I have included this section again. If you have already read this part feel free to skip it. If not, below is an explanation of white light.

Everybody knows about white light. Our human explanation is that it is a light which contains all the wavelengths of the visible spectrum. In a spiritual context, it is more than all the colors contained in one. White light is a versatile light that can be used for various purposes.

We can channel in white light as part of our healing practice. As it contains all the colors, it is like covering all the bases. Every color is available for use, as all are contained in the one light. Beginners normally use white light when starting their healing journey.

The light not only protects us, but also can lessen any energetic drainage. Enclosed in our bubble others can't drain us so easily. I "white light" myself in any draining environment. Hospitals and shopping centers are particularly bad; in fact, anywhere there are large groups of people I cover myself with light before entering. As mentioned in "Spiritual Answers for Health and Happiness," talking on the phone can also drain us. So before I answer I try to always white light myself because we never know who is calling.

Sometimes, we may instinctively need more layers of light. This occurs with very draining people or places. I recommend that you put on extra layers when a situation becomes more tiring, maybe three or four more. If you are spending more time than usual in a place or are with someone who is very draining, extra light might be necessary. Just do what feels right. I have actually stood in front of people adding more and more layers. They will be totally unaware of what is happening in front of their eyes.

The more we use these methods, the easier it becomes. Eventually, it will become a habit. These days I rarely forget to white light myself. If I do forget, it takes only a thought to set things right.

White light can also be used for psychic protection. You can cover your aura with light; this is called "white lighting" yourself. When we leave the house and want to be protected from other energies, we can visualize white light covering our entire energy body. The light serves as an interface between us and the external energy world, like a raincoat of light. We can also white light other people. In white lighting them, we send protection to them. It could be at their workplace, for their plane flight, their holiday or when they are ill. We can white light animals too. I once watched a koala running across a very busy road and immediately white lighted her to give extra protection. Happily, she made it safely across.

Before driving off people white light their cars. On transit from here to there it provides added protection. Sometimes, I have forgotten and been reminded to do it. Several times soon after one of these reminders, a near miss happened. Our angels will often remind us about white lighting if we forget. When light is sent as protection, we need to be aware that it can only do so much. I have heard complaints about the light not stopping a car crash happening, etc. Try to understand that if the person or persons involved had already decided on the soul level that the car crash had to occur for certain learning or karma, the light won't stop it. What it may do is minimize the damage.

I remember my friend was about to use our car. He was a new, fairly inexperienced driver. On the morning, I had a bad feeling about him driving. I tried to encourage him to use the bus, but he was having none of it. So off he went. All day, I felt uneasy, and kept white lighting the car. At three o'clock the call came. He had hit another car at the traffic lights. The car contained two people in their eighties, and their car had been pushed through the intersection and had crashed into a massive electrical transformer. When I arrived there were police cars, the fire-engine, two ambulances and two, very badly crashed vehicles. The traffic was being diverted as the firemen cut the old lady out of the crushed car. I was totally shocked. Luckily, my friend, the older man and his wife were all unscathed. Although I could not prevent the crash, the white light sent protected them all. One of the witnesses even commented that the angels were looking after them that day. Never underestimate the power of the spiritual world. Remember, that even when some event needs to occur, there is always room to assist its final outcome.

White light can also be sent to places in chaos elsewhere in the world. The light will quicken the healing process. People we have never met can also be sent light to protect them from attack or assassination. The world is a place of chance; any light sent to places in turmoil will assist in some way. It is never a waste to send light.

In conclusion, we need to understand that while we may cover ourselves with light that it will never block our aura. Like glass, it only serves to protect and shield us, and we will continue to be as accessible to others as before.

Rainbow light

While white light contains the hues visible to the human eye, rainbow light has a different combination. This light includes all these colors and more. I liken it to the multi-vitamin pill of the lights because our aura is nourished with all these colors. At times of stress, the rainbow light fills up any empty tanks around the energy body. When you access rainbow light remember it will contain more colors than you know on earth. With this awareness, you can access these extra hues, and in doing so, your aura will vibrate on a higher level.

With more rainbow-colored light in our aura, we become more radiant. People tend to respond by telling us how well we look. Without realizing it, they are picking up on the lights. As souls, we all read and recognize the various lights in someone's aura. Rainbow light is valuable to access when we need an extra boost. Bring it into your aura like the other lights. All you have to do is ask. It is good to send to others whom you feel may benefit from it. The aura constantly repairs itself and so by filling it up with these rainbow lights, we can be sure of supplying some of the missing pieces.

I feel the rainbow light, full with so many hues, is a valuable addition to our energy body, so remember to use it when appropriate.

Gold light

Gold holds great power in our world physically and psychically. Just as gold is a precious mineral in our human world, so is it in the spiritual realms. Healers and light workers use gold frequently to repair and seal areas because channeling in gold strengthens the aura both physically and spiritually. In healing practice it is common knowledge that gold light resonates on a very high level. Gold signifies the Oneness of all there is. Our aura will vibrate closer to the God Light when it contains more gold.

Gold light is not merely a gold color. Deep in its structure are cells aligned with the core of the universal light. The essence of gold is held in these cells, as it is part of the building blocks of all there is. This has positive outcomes when we bring gold light into our aura. Running this light through the energy body seals and strengthens us in a way that other lights may not do. It is the mother of light so to speak.

When we explore history, we always see gold viewed with similar reverence. Throughout the ages, most religions used gold extensively. I believe that for us on the earth plane gold is the closest vibration to the Oneness, to God.

As mentioned earlier, in spiritual work gold light is perfect for healing, sealing areas and reinforcing the aura, as well as protecting the skin of the aura. It has such a depth and potency that a little goes a long way. Plus, gold gives emotional, mental and spiritual strength when needed. Sending gold light to others during difficult times will steady and nourish them. Furthermore, with more gold in our aura, our own spiritual growth can be heightened as drawing it in enables us to resonate closer to the higher realms, and consequently, the connection for both sides becomes easier.

Filling up your energy body with gold will definitely strengthen you. You can visualize bringing gold light into your aura, and aim to wear gold-colored clothing and gold jewelry. Sunshine is another easy way to access gold. Sunlight vibrates similar golden hues, which in turn feed our aura.

Gold transcends time and space. This light is unique, a precious light, the essence of universal light.

Silver light

Silver light radiates much healing and has a strengthening quality similar to the metal. It can support and give structure to the energy grid. It is beneficial to draw silver into the aura when antibiotic healing is required as it is king among the lights for viral and bacterial infections. During a nasty throat infection, I was guided to bring in silver light. Sometimes, when I follow my messages, I don't know the reason why; however, in this case it became clear the following day. It was silver's antibiotic quality I needed.

Silver light vibrates at a particular rate and cleanses as it moves through the aura. I believe it has the ability to concentrate in certain areas. For example, if the lungs are affected a concentration of silver light will settle there. If the infection is in the foot, the same process occurs. The site of the problem attracts the silver light. It has a sterile quality, yet untapped here on earth.

Use it when you have any infection or immune problem. Its antiseptic nature will assist by shortening the illness and clearing out the debris. Silver is like the sea as it washes and removes toxins and energy from the aura. In addition, past-life residue left in the aura can be sterilized and cleansed in this way.

Like gold, consider wearing silver on your person to access its qualities and using colloidal silver to support your body.

Silver is a wonderful light to use when deep cleansing of the energy body is required.

Violet light

Of all the lights violet seems to be the one connected to the Christ Consciousness. All through the ages, the violet light has been linked with religion and spirituality, almost like a cord of light to God and universal love. Violet light is of this world and particularly the spiritual realms; it is the color corresponding to the crown chakra. I feel that we have only now begun to fathom the enormity of this light.

In violet comes the divinity vibration. This light holds healing and, at times, curing abilities. By imagining our aura filled with violet will not only help in our spiritual ascension, but shift blocks and illnesses. There is a depth in this light underpinning its power. Some call it the violet flame, and like a flame, it has variations and qualities unlike other lights. Violet cleanses in an amazing way; moving through the aura it gently, but strongly, releases unwanted energies.

Violet represents purity of soul, and by cleansing with violet light we connect again with the higher part of ourselves.

Our pureness of being is renewed. The more violet light that we have in our being, the higher we can vibrate. It also has the strength of steel. It is an ethereal light, one of the lights closest to God.

Use it with the intention to give love and peace to others. Bathe yourself in it regularly. Fill yourself down to a cellular level with violet, for remember, each cell is a mini-version of the aura. You will find this work will assist with your spiritual aspirations. Visualize it, surround yourself with the physical color and burn or wear violet essence. I like to rub violet oil on my third eye and on the top of my lip. The smell sense is one of our strongest and least recognized gifts; therefore, by infusing ourselves in its light, we absorb it on all levels.

Many believe violet light can heighten our concentration while meditating. These people use a violet-colored lamp or let the light shine through a pane of purple glass when meditating. I believe that is why churches have leadlight windows. The light shining through the glass affects us by strengthening our connection to God.

I have always thought violet has a mysterious quality to it. When I look into the violet color, it feels like I could fall into its light and be absorbed into it. Being such an intense color it seems to hold a power about it.

Pink light

I always send pink light when love is needed as this color resonates well with the heart. I know some psychics believe there are green hues around the heart chakra, but I see pink there as well. Anyone in love or working with love will radiate this light in his or her aura. In the olden days, pink was supposed to be for girls and blue for boys. An old-fashioned notion. We all know that pink represents the softness of our feminine side.

Although not a female light, it contains the female aspects of us, for we are a mixture of male and feminine energy.

We can always use pink light, especially when extra love is needed. It softens and calms a stressed energy body and during emotional turmoil the extra pink reinforces the heart chakra acting like a medicine for the heart. This light supports us emotionally and, in my experience, most people can easily access pink. I have sent this light directly to the heart chakra, and put people in a huge bubble of pink light. The bubble protects and strengthens them in these times of need. All you have to do is to imagine the other person standing in a bubble of pink. Next, visualize them happy and at peace.

Before operations and during illness, pink is a valuable light to send. It can support any damage in the aura and help the healing to progress more smoothly. If the person concerned wishes to cross over, pink softens the transition by alleviating much of the fear.

Animals are very receptive to pink light. Our cord to them is essentially based on love, so they are already open to receiving. I have sent pink light to various animals, birds and fish around the globe. As a rule, during world disasters the animals, birds and sea life are sadly neglected.

We can send pink light to needy places around the world. It helps to cushion the outcomes and enables higher-frequency energies to flow into these areas. Coming from the heart chakra, pink encompasses our human and spiritual aspects. When we have more pink in our energy body, the easier it will be for us to move ahead in peace. Anger, fear and hate may be released more easily when the aura is full of pink.

Everyone is capable of sending pink light, and because it vibrates close to the love band imagine how much more love and peace our world could have if we all sent this light. Sending pink light, like love, has a power we are only beginning to understand. As the human race advances spiritually, the love energy will emerge as our greatest gift. Hopefully, in this era its healing power will be understood and spiritual growth in our world will be limitless.

With love, I believe the best is yet to come.

Moonlight light

The "moonlight people" know who they are. There are many of them here at this time. During the centuries, the moonlight has held a fascination for many people. Shamans, priestesses and medicine doctors all knew about its magical power. In addition, its power is well-acknowledged in witchcraft practices. However, in this section, I am not referring directly to the human concept of the moonlight. I am writing about the moonlight from an energetic perspective.

The moonlight directly affects our lives for, as it waxes and wanes, it alters every living thing. The moon is connected to our emotional energy. I believe that we all vibrate to the heartbeat of the moon. This close connection has implications, for we are all little versions of the moon in a vibrational sense. Knowing this innate correlation explains our instinctive response to the full moon as it is encoded in our aura from the beginning of our time on the earth plane.

There is a grounding aspect to the moonlight. It is our energetic heartbeat, our earthing device. Every living creature is in sync with the moon. Police and hospital workers may laugh at the last idea. Nevertheless, it is well-known that many people display very bizarre and often unstable behavior around the full moon. The reason this occurs has less to do with the moon and more to do with the imbalance in the person's aura. I believe that their aura and the moon's aura actually clash, hence the crazy outbursts. It is like music. If the band and I are both in tune, we harmonize and add to each other. On the other hand, once we vibrate at different rates, our music will clash. So it is with the moon's light and us. Although the light coming from the moon is not really from the physical moon, it carries the moon's aura, its vibration.

We can bring in the moonlight whenever we have the need. All we need to do is to draw in its energy. Sitting outside and basking in the moonlight has a similar outcome. The moon has a cleansing quality for our planet as it shines upon us. It is healing because it grounds us and connects us to earth. Once we begin to bring this energy into our aura, we can benefit energetically. I believe it is wonderful to meditate in moonlight and that our psychic senses are heightened by its light.

We are part of the moon, and the moon is part of us. Through time and space, we are all connected at the deepest level. Cherish, access and enjoy the moon's beauty.

Sunlight light

Everyone knows the importance of sunlight. Without it, we would die and without enough of it can become ill and depressed. Sunshine makes us happy.

There is another aspect energetically. Sunlight carries its own code, energy we have not fully begun to tap into. Solar power is just the beginning. Our aura is definitely affected by the sunlight. All living beings can absorb and convert sunlight. It has a similar quality to the brilliant light on the other side. The sun radiates the essence of other dimensions, the golden quality permeating through everything.

We can absorb sunlight directly and indirectly. We already know this in our world. Sitting in the direct light will feed our aura. Even sitting inside with the sun shining into a room will allow us to absorb much light.

The sunlight has other yet unknown facets. Lights within lights, we can't yet measure.

Earth light

Earth energy is used every day keeping us grounded. When you access this slower, heavier light you can feel the difference. It is solid and thick, and when I work with it, I can sense its slow, whirling quality. Most healers use this light to balance and ground themselves and others. When we are spacey and floating off, this heavy, dense light helps the aura to settle down. I bring it in when I feel ungrounded and disconnected from my human reality.

Essentially, the more spiritual work we do, the more necessary it is to ground ourselves. When our vibration quickens, it becomes lighter, so it is easy to live in the clouds. This lightness can mean we can become ungrounded very easily. The earth light will add some weight, so to speak, to our aura and help to balance us. The yin and yang balance is important in energetic terms. When our aura is balanced, we are balanced too. On a personal level, it benefits us, and as a healer/reader it keeps us well.

I visualize pulling the slow earth energy up through my feet. You can infuse your aura this way and then send the earth light to others. The animal kingdom knows the importance of this energy. While they are lying on the ground and resting, they are drawing the energy into their bodies. Tribal people spend time sitting on the ground. However, people in our modern societies don't sit and connect with the earth like that very often. We have lost a natural instinctive way of drawing earth energy into our auras. Take time to sit on the grass and bring in the light. By sitting on the ground, we can draw the light up into our base chakra and up to our crown. It only takes a few minutes to refill. Some "sensitives" can literally feel the slow vibration traveling up through their bodies.

In drawing up this positive earth light, we can release any negative light and ask it to be returned in good faith to the earth.

Celestial light

Celestial light comes from higher dimensions and it is a special light that we are able to draw down. Its vibration is higher and finer than we have on earth, yet I feel we are able to access it easily. Messages and healings benefit when we run this light as it carries information. By accessing the light, we can raise our aural rate.

I have used it throughout my time as a healer/reader. This fine light is a valuable tool in assisting the removal of heavy energy. As it moves through the aura, it can shift the trapped energies out from our energy grid. I believe that bringing in this particular light will quicken our vibrational rate and expand our psychic knowledge. With the higher frequencies allowing us to ascend spiritually, our soul can reach higher planes. With a substantially stronger soul vibration, the human part of us will benefit. This light keeps the aura less prone to illness and lower frequency drainage.

You can bring it in whenever you need higher access, or before you do any spiritual work.

Laser light

This light is particularly used for healing. I can sense when my spiritual healers are using this concentrated laser light. Some healers are skilled at using this light, but it takes practice.

Normally, laser is used in healing when spiritual operations are taking place. Energy can be cut out and removed with laser light techniques. Afterwards, higher-frequency light can be used to fill the area.

Laser is a known practice in our society, yet it is less recognized in healing work. You can ask to use this method, as knowing about it will open doors to higher and varied healing skills for you and those you work on. During the healing, it can feel like the work is selectively burning into the person's aura. I was initially nervous about using such a concentration of light, in case I made a mistake. Obviously, that was my ego kicking in. I suggest you ask for clear guidance and give the process over to your spiritual helpers. In my earlier days, there were times I would feel that the work was finished and move on. I would then be told to go back because they weren't finished yet. It was a valuable lesson for me in working with Spirit.

Try not to be afraid of using laser light. Those working with us spiritually have backup plans if we move at the wrong time or make a mistake. Frequently, when using the light the person we are working on may comment on the intensity of heat. They may feel the burning quality of the heat, as it builds up very quickly and cuts deep into their aura.

Some people use crystals to enhance their laser work. You will be guided if this path is for you. Follow your instincts. During healings we are only the channels. By acknowledging the laser light, you will be open to its use. This new awareness means it can be incorporated into future healings, which will be a bonus for your spiritual growth and for your recipient.

Cleansing light

A light I had not realized we could access was the cleansing light. When I was fighting off a virus, I had used the silver light, particularly at the start. However, during an illness, many toxins are being released. Illness is normally the body's way of doing a big clean out, like resetting the body health clock. Towards the end of my short sickness, I was advised to wash through my aura with the cleansing light. It was then I knew that this light was specifically for cleaning. In the process, this light was collecting extra energies and, like a broom, sweeping them from the energy body. Like other lights, it moves through and out of the energy body.

When I worked with this light I mainly brought it in from my head and washed it out through my feet. During my illness, I just used the light whenever I felt I needed to cleanse.

We all know to drink more fluids with colds and flu. It helps the physical body clean and remove toxins. The light was doing the same. When I did the wash, it felt like a sea shower to me. On a color scale, I saw it like water, full of shimmering mother-of-pearl colors. It seemed fluid and dense with a myriad of colors. This light was not to refill or change the aural structure, for its sole purpose was to collect debris and wash the energy field. It was like the illness dislodged the unnecessary energies, and the light picked them up and disposed of them. Needless to say, my flu cleared up more quickly than usual.

Many times we clear out on all levels. Viruses and flu are mostly about physical, emotional and mental release. Therefore, it is important to support ourselves with the cleansing light. Using this technique strengthens our body. I ran the light through for several days after the virus had passed, as I knew the body was still in the process of cleaning up.

When you are feeling unwell you can use the light too. Many illnesses are caused by blockages, and it is worthwhile to run this light.

You may wonder why you should not just run white light through. I used to think in the same way. Still, as we develop and hone our skills, we need to be more selective. It is better to use the best light for each occasion. Yes, we can use a generic light that will possibly cover it, but given the perfect light, why settle for less?

The cleansing light is an unusual light with special powers. Keep it in mind when you are seeking a cleanse on the physical, emotional, mental and spiritual level.

Colors around the globe

The world has its own aura with colors swirling throughout it. Some areas around the world are rich in some colors, while others are not. These globe colors are influenced by the world's energetic aura. It is also directly influenced by the energies residing in these places, and with this knowing we can understand why the world is like it is.

Our aura has colors and chakras, and the globe has the same. When scientists speak about the ozone hole, they are referring to the aural energy hole. These holes around the world are causing energy leakage. They are not like portals that open and close. The globe has a sheath around it just like our eggshell skin, and any breaks around the sheath cause damage.

Around the world, there are countries with different hues. When I first saw it psychically I was thinking about Italy and I "saw" it swathed in blue light. Europe appears green, while the Americas are predominately orange and yellow. The islands have lighter hues of turquoise and red in certain places. Africa is red and yellow. I could "see" that the further north and south I went the cleaner and lighter the blue was. The seas are a green blue, while the forests and woods take on a light silver color. Extraordinary! There were pockets of light according to who was living there and the vegetation or lack of it. When we plant more trees and make wetlands for birds it directly changes the aural colors of the area. So working on greening our planet and maintaining fresh waterways will impact upon it enormously. How wonderful the healing is for the soul of Mother Earth!

The thought patterns and negativity of the people located in parts of the world impact on its hue. Positive actions and thoughts improve the colors, yet negative actions and outmoded thinking muddies and dulls the brilliance of the lights. When I channeled this information, I was surprised, but it all made sense.

There are billions of us trying to heal the world and alter the globe's aura. We can plant, clean and beautify our own small patch. We can send light so each place can access more. There is so much we can do. We have only to explore these possibilities.

Colored lights from other dimensions

When people cross over to the other side and return they talk about the beautiful colored lights. I believe many of these colors are being "downloaded" to our earth plane at this time. Advanced beings working here know how to draw these lights into our world. They have worked with these lights in other dimensions, and their energy body can easily accommodate them. You can ask to be given access to the spiritual lights as they can be transferred to us. In addition, having these extra hues in our world enables us to tap into new areas of learning.

Light carries information, and even if we can't see these lights with our eyes they are there. It is hard to comprehend lights if we have never seen them with our human eyes. However, remember, we have seen them before with our soul eyes. It is through our soul that the lights can activate on earth. These lights carry energy from other dimensions. They act as a connection from one dimension to another.

The colors and dimensional quality of these lights are foreign to our human eyes, not our souls. As we will be accessing them on a soul wavelength, they will be easily accommodated into our aura because we are all more than our human shell.

Be open and receiving when it comes to the spiritual lights. Our earth is vibrating at a higher rate. Therefore, our auras are too.

Black light

Few books write about the black light, but where there is light, there will be dark. Just as white light has a power and strength, so does the black. On some level, we have already accepted the concept of black light existing in our earthly realm. In the science world, humans ponder on the existence of black holes. To me, black holes have a mystery and sacredness too.

The black light I write about is not only a color, but also an energy made of light. I know it seems like a contradiction to speak of light and black in the same sentence, but all is light. Black light is necessary to balance the universe. It brings with it comfort and grounding.

I believe that this light can alter the aura by filling areas and virtually creating space. For black light's gift is the space it provides and so where space is needed this light is invaluable. To be honest, even though I know what I have written to be true, I don't totally understand the process. My sense is that, like the black holes, this light provides a type of vacuum that we are still unaware of. Maybe in the future we will all come to understand how black light works and how it can benefit our aura. When I tune in to this light, it feels like comfort or protection is given, yet I don't know much more.

In the decades to come black light will come into its own. Very little is known about its attributes now, but given time we will begin to tap into its greatness.

Brilliant white Light from the other side

Most of us have heard of the brilliant white Light on the other side. Some of us who have crossed and returned have seen it. When I crossed the Light was incredibly white and amazingly bright. Everyone speaks of the Light in the same way. For me, it was white, brilliant and opaque. The Light spreads out endlessly, and I could not actually see into it. Although it was shining with such intensity, it did not hurt my eyes. I wondered why, as all who saw the Light had similar observations. Then it dawned on me.

Of course, I was looking through my eyes as a soul, not as a human. Having crossed into this dimension I had temporarily left my human form at home, so to speak. No wonder we can gaze upon it without squinting or being blinded, for we don't use our normal human senses. As we are in soul mode, we view the Light with our soul eyes. It was the same concept as when I spoke with my deceased mother, and we used telepathy to speak, not the human voice.

I believe the white Light leads us home. It draws us back like a beacon, lest we become lost when we cross. If we were to see into the Light we would realize the whiteness masks the swirling colors it contains. For white is made of all colors.

The Light also contains love and calmness. It radiates warmth and peace. Once touched by the Light our life will never be the same again. In most mystical experiences, the

Light is the common thread. Whether it was experienced by Moses, Saint Bernadette or simply the lady down the street, the brilliant white Light remains the same.

The Light is not bound by time and space. It is never-ending and can cross all dimensions.

Some Personal Issues

Never follow a guru or walk upon their feet. Listen and learn from the teacher, but make your own footprints in the path of life.

Protecting yourself

Once we embark on the light work, we will need to use methods to keep our own aura safe. With all spiritual endeavors, you work by using your aura as the vehicle. As the conduit, your energy body is directly involved, so it is important that you set protection in place. Before I read the cards or do a healing, I cover myself with light and ask for protection. I visualize being in a bubble of white light. In this bubble, I can work knowing that my personal energy field will be safe.

There will be times in the healing work when you are virtually dragging pain from a person's aura through your aura. Regularly, you can feel it in your own hands or body. It is good the pain is being released. Nevertheless, it is important their energy does not lodge in your aura.

This is where the protection does its work. The light will allow the healing to be done, while keeping you safe. Once I stop working, I wash my aura with white light. If it is necessary, I do it a couple of times. Next, I cut any energetic cords remaining from me to the client. This part is very important. If the cords remain, these people will be able to access us energetically. Energy connections, once in place, can last for ages. If you forget to protect yourself, then do it as soon as you remember. Similarly, if you forget to wash and cut, just do that as soon as possible.

On a physical level I wash my hands. A few times, I have felt compelled to wash up to my elbows. Rarely, I have had a complete shower and washed my hair. Remember to follow your own feelings after a healing or reading. If you have never worked like this, please don't panic. Just do a general light cover, wash and cut from all those you have worked on.

It is great to help others, but it is counterproductive to be drained by everyone. In the end, you won't be as effective on a personal or professional level.

Some healers use their own removal techniques, visualizing the excess energy being put in baskets and taken away by Spirit. Others see the energy being converted into various positive things and being returned to the universe. It does not matter what method you choose. The significant part is white lighting your aura, cleaning yourself and disconnecting from the client's energy.

Initially, I felt a little uncomfortable cutting the cords, especially with the people I really liked. At the beginning, you might find it extremely difficult with your partner, children and close friends. Somehow, it feels rude and unkind. However, as I progressed, I recognized the importance of this practice. It was unhealthy for me to be attached energetically to their aura. From the other point of view, it was not healthy for them to continue to be connected to my energy.

Once we begin to use these practices our work can advance, and we won't be heading for burnout. With a healthy energy field, our abilities will be heightened, which will be a great outcome for all concerned.

Healing choices

To be a good channel you need to be unselfish about the work. There will be times it feels inconvenient to you, and you may feel disinterested or distracted. In spite of this, if you listen to your feelings, there will be occasions when you know that the work has to be done now. With these healings/readings, you may have to put your own needs aside. Whether you take up the call to do it or not, the choice is still always yours.

I have found my urge to work under these circumstances is undeniably strong. In a sense, I can't ignore it, and I always end up fulfilling my calling. For universal work comes from the deep calling within. I have found Spirit always supports me through these times. I have had situations when I knew I had to do my duty. Maybe I was the only healer/channel available at the time. It needed to be done. In these cases, I asked for help and extra healing strength. Spirit will always give us support. There will be time later to rest and finish what was put aside.

Following guidance without question takes great faith. In our world of reason, we are used to working in a rational manner, while with spiritual endeavors we rely on our feelings and instinct. So next time you have a similar situation, follow your feelings.

Service work is sorely needed on earth. Believe in your own gifts and use your abilities to assist others. It is not always easy to put yourself out, but it is a true test of faith and a divine use of your gift.

Working when we are tired

We all know that we are not as clear when tired. Frequently, we can become cranky and make easy mistakes. However, in our quest to do the spiritual work, we can become blind to this happening to us. When we are tired, our psychic gifts can be affected. On a good day, the information will flow easily and without effort, but tiredness dulls the gift, and our clarity and ability to focus will be compromised.

I was not always aware of my tiredness. We can become used to being tired and not actually recognize it. Those around us can more easily identify tiredness in us. My left eyelid tends to droop when I am too tired, so if I don't register my fatigue, others will let me know.

As a reader and healer there will regularly be demands on your time. Upset and confused people don't think about where you are in the picture because their focus will be on themselves. Remember, a good time for them may not necessarily be a good time for you. Be firm if you feel you are too tired to channel or do healings. If you are pressed for a psychic answer, ask them to leave it with you. After being rested, you may be able to connect properly and access the answer.

Tiredness will fog your aura and can affect your focus. We are all human with our own lives and lessons, so sacrificing our health helps no one and compromises the gift.

An added consideration is to be aware of the lesson for the person. As mentioned earlier, there are times the message does not come because the person has to go through the experience for his or her own learning. Be aware of this scenario.

Remember, that no guidance is better than poor guidance.

Working when we are upset

Tapping into our feelings is how we connect with Spirit. Reading the cards, healing work or getting messages primarily focuses on how it feels. When we are balanced, we can be very clear, but if our emotional body is upset it can directly influence our ability to channel. Clarity depends on a good, clear connection, and a good, clear connection depends on us being in balance. If I am a mess emotionally, how can I channel properly? It would be like trying to find clarity in a muddy pool.

We use our feelings, not our mind to channel. If we listen to our spiritual healings/readings we use terms like, "I feel" and "I sense." I rarely use the analytical part of my mind. I might hear the messages or words in my mind. However, I use my emotions to connect with my guardians.

So remember to be aware of where you are emotionally when you channel. If you are upset it can directly affect your abilities. Unfortunately, you can unwittingly tap into fear and doubt, and negative emotions on your part can compromise a good reading. Everyone has bad days. Some of us have bad weeks. Don't be pressured into working through these times. Keep in mind the saying that "a rest is as good as a holiday."

If I receive a message from other readers when they are in an emotional mess, I don't take for granted their clarity. Like you, their own muddy waters can affect the messages.

There is great responsibility when we channel for others. People can hang on to our every word. I believe others deserve to get the best we can give, so abstain from channeling through emotional upheavals. If pressed you can choose to channel, but explain your position. I have still been pretty clear even on chaotic days, but the other person needs to understand we are doing the best on a bad day.

On a personal level, it can be too taxing. There are days when I screen my calls and checkout. Nowadays, I know my limits and don't push them.

Emotional distress compromises our channeling. It is worse than being sick. Listen to your own instincts and allow yourself time-out. It is always better to have no message, than an incorrect one.

Working when we are ill

It is never a good idea to work when we are ill. Unfortunately, our society supports the "soldier on" attitude. In daily life, we can cope with some occupations when we have a crashing headache or the flu. However, light work is different.

There will be several reasons not to work. Obviously, if it is a contagious virus, we should not infect others. We can easily reschedule, and the client will appreciate our consideration. People hate it when they turn up to any occasion and others sneeze and cough all over them.

It can be tempting to ignore feeling sick and try to work through it. Maybe, it is a long-standing pattern of doing the right thing, and working through it all. On other occasions, we might actually need the money to buy basics like food and pay bills. However, never work only for the money. Have faith as Spirit will frequently send some material help in the following weeks.

Often, illness is a sign of the aura doing a big clean out. In general, negative emotions are coming to the surface to be released, and toxins around the aura are being removed. It requires energy to do these clearings, and your body needs to use its own energy to complete the process. Recognize when you are shifting out unwanted energies and need a break. Allow yourself to lie on the couch and watch television. Get off the world roundabout until you are better. By resting, the cleanse will be more effective, and you can get through it quickly. Relax and let the time be just for you.

I noticed that at each new spiritual level I manifested this kind of release. To ascend, I needed to vibrate higher, so I had to experience clearing on all layers.

When we are sick, the aura is unbalanced, and trying to work when we are like this stresses the aura much more. It's like trying to run in the race when you have twisted your ankle. Your performance is always compromised. I want my sessions to be the best they can be. I want the other person to get value for the time we work together. For me, the quality must be there.

As a vibrating being, I should be running at a faster rate than my client, in order for me to channel the best light. My recipient should not be running higher than me. The reason is simple. The higher energy overrides the lower. They are coming for the healing/reading, and the flow should be from the channel to them, not the reverse.

Of course, there are particular people who come to us and vibrate at a very high rate. I know them before they even arrive because before I begin the session, I am instructed to raise my vibrational rate. Being sick means you aren't vibrating at your usual level, and when you are ill, it is hard to bring your rate up.

On a purely human level, you may need to ask yourself why you aren't putting yourself first. As light workers we can fall into the role of rescuer, and all those service lives can make us self-sacrificing. Old patterns run deep in the soul body. You are the most important person in your life, and in valuing yourself and your time, you teach others to do, likewise.

In a society bent on pleasing and seeking approval it is important to make your own personal list of do's and don'ts. Listen to your own body and gut feelings. Ask your body what it needs. Cancel appointments and screen your phone calls when unwell. The world keeps spinning, and when we finally rejoin the human race, not much has changed.

I have observed an interesting aspect to the healing/reading work. Once I began to honor myself and canceled sessions when ill or upset, another pattern began to emerge. While I was sick, nothing happened. The phone stopped ringing, and no one wanted to come during these days or weeks. It was like I had disappeared for a while. Then once I began to get better, everything came back to normal. In a sense, I had created my own reality. My actions had changed my physical reality. The phone ringing again heralded the end was coming. I found that there was comfort in the whole process.

Working with the Light is an honor and a gift. In serving yourself and taking good care of your health, you show respect and reverence for the Light. Remember that although we are souls of light, we reside in a dense, physical human form. Our guardians want us to take good care of ourselves here on earth.

Power naps

Power naps are a useful way to recharge the aura. This type of nap does not actually involve going to sleep. With the power nap, you concentrate and connect into the spiritual realm. I use power naps to access more energy and balance my aura.

All I do is find a quiet place where I won't be disturbed. Next, I relax and tune into the universal energy. I request that my aura be filled with the necessary light. It is useful to power nap before you do any spiritual work. There will be times when the thought of working seems like an effort because we feel slower than normal. Perhaps we have a client who might be hard to work with, so bringing in this additional light will enable us to breeze through a difficult session.

I use power naps for my daily life. A short, energy charge makes the rest of the day go well. There have been times when I did doze off. Don't worry if this happens to you, as it does not mean you weren't concentrating or doing it correctly. Some days the physical body just needs more sleep. You can power nap on the bus, or while waiting for someone. I found that the more I napped, the easier the process became.

We can also send power naps to others, so they can access the energy. I visualize them and see the energy filling their aura. The extra boost can help them through tough times.

Keeping well hydrated

Anyone who works with energy knows the importance of water. Our bodies are mostly made of water. Therefore, using our body to channel and convey healing means the amount of water in our system is important. We need to keep our fluids up when doing energy work. Obviously, a well-hydrated body will be healthier and allow us to do the light work with less stress on us. It is possible to work when we are dehydrated, but it will directly affect the healing outcome. Vibrating at a high level will be harder to achieve, besides the fact that water is paramount to feeling balanced and focused.

The energy we channel in runs through our body. That means it runs through the water in our body. Everyone knows that water is a great conductor of energy. This makes it even more important to keep well hydrated when channeling.

I suggest that you drink a lot of water for good health, and especially if you want to do light work. To enhance the energetic quality of your water you can put crystals in the water jugs. Some people activate the water by putting it into colored glass containers, and in that way, the vibrations of the color are absorbed. Sunlight and moonlight also affect the water energetically. I have held the glass in my two hands and channeled light into the water. It is interesting to check the water with a pendulum before you channel and then afterwards. You will see a difference.

During healings water, especially excess water, can be felt. As the dampness releases from the aura, I can feel it in my hands. It feels like a sauna, especially if there is some heat as well. I noticed that too much trapped water can literally slow down some areas in the body and cause bloating. Normally, people who don't drink enough can experience this phenomenon. Some people believe our body, being depleted, holds on to as much water as it can, which in turn causes the bloating or puffiness. This is an interesting observation.

Water is healing and a cleanser. It cleans the physical body and the energetic one. People instinctively know that water heals. When tense, tired or needing direction they are led to water. The yearning to walk on the beach, lie in the bath or be near water becomes compelling.

We are the water. It is the same energy. So the answers we seek for ourselves are also in the water. When we gaze at a calm sea or tranquil lake, I feel that the water inside of us stills too. We become as one.

Water is our friend. Mother Earth has provided it for us, so use it wisely.

Water as a channel

Being around water heightens channeling for many of us. When I first started it was a feature of the spiritual work I did not understand. However, while involved in water activities, I would receive messages and psychic pictures for others and myself. It could happen in the shower, while washing the dishes and sometimes while in the bathroom. I would laugh as I told someone I saw this picture when I was in these very ordinary places. Gradually, I noticed that the common link was the water, any contact with water.

Our spiritual connection is enhanced greatly via the water, as it becomes a conduit between the two worlds. Water supports the travel of universal energy. Therefore, when we are close to water, our psychic skills are enhanced. It acts like an amplifier. On a level, we all recognize this because when lost and confused, we head to water. It is an intuitive knowing.

Another aspect is the trance-like quality water can have on us. Washing is not only grounding. The contact with water can also put us into a receptive frame of mind. Once we are engaged in our little water trance, Spirit can contact us more easily. I think water opens up portals to other dimensions. I have received numerous insights when doing mundane water-based chores. Therefore, never underestimate these activities for they are like little water meditations.

Water has long been used for healing and spiritual work. Gazing into ponds or bowls of water have been ways for clairvoyants to access messages and gain guidance. While meditation requires time and space and a particular focus, water channeling happens while the world passes us by. Happily relaxing in the bath or washing the car, the information pops into our mind. It seems these mundane, almost repetitive activities are similar to the state that we find ourselves in when we meditate. I suggest that you ask to be open to receive in this way. When I am around water, I try to be an open channel to my guides. With this intention, you will be amazed how many insights come to you.

It is in its simplicity that the greatest insights can be found. I believe that in being as one with the water, our strongest connection is made. The door is ever open to the universe.

People being scared of us

When people find out you are a medium, reader or healer they can be scared of you. Someone told me I was scary because I could read their mind, however, nothing can be further from the truth. It is normal to encounter these reactions. So take heart. These days I can feel when others around me are nervous, as I sense their fear. Perhaps you may have felt their fear too. Try not to focus on their emotion. Be normal and reassure them that you are like them. Well, nearly! I like to think of myself like Wendy with an extra bit. When I am with someone who displays fear, I highlight my humanness and put my psychic part to the side.

Humans always fear what they can't understand. It is a natural survival instinct. However, I want to help others to understand how the human and spiritual sides can come together, and scaring them won't work. When I am with these people, I keep the conversation normal by talking about topics everyone is comfortable with. If the subject of my gift comes up, I try not to engage in too many explanations about these abilities.

People's fear comes from ideas about witches, spells and magic, but the spiritual journey I am on has been little to do with that. The religious ones may believe we are working with the devil, or that we are the devil in disguise. I had many religious friends praying for my salvation. It was ironic as I had been to God's heaven, spoken with the angels and come back. People are strange really!

No one likes to feel set apart in company, yet it happens. Just be yourself and don't buy into their fear. The more normal you are, the better the outcomes. As they become more comfortable in your space, everyone can relax. By and large, once people come to realize we are similar to them, they are more open. Then, if some message or picture comes to you, telling them may be easier. However, always be aware that they may have a wall of protection up, so respect it. In these situations, I don't push the point too much.

More often, we may have to adjust to them. While writing these books, I only spoke about the books in a general way. I kept it short and within everyone's comfort zone. If I had discussed any of the real chapters in the books, these individuals would have been heading for the door.

I believe this is my path, my journey. Each of us can be with others, yet walk quite different paths. Luckily, in life, we can find those friends with whom we can be our whole selves, and I treasure these friendships. They are the jewels in our lives. In general, I found adjusting to others to allay their fears is the choice I make. It is not devaluing who I am. It is being aware of where everyone is in the big picture, and acting accordingly.

Filtering

Once we embark upon our journey, we may be used as a filter. By this I mean that we use our aura to filter through energy. We are all energy, so filtering energy through our aura is automatic. Everyone does it daily. Just being in the world means we are constantly exchanging energy. As light workers we act as filters. Energy in the form of thoughts, pain and emotions are passing through our auras with many of us acting like big, cleaning machines.

On a world level, lots of us are filtering fear and anger via our auras. It can be a conscious act. People know they are clearing world problems and those who do soul rescue are very aware of it. However, many are not sure why they are feeling fear and anger. Without being aware, they are also picking up world feelings and processing them. These individuals will feel the emotions, but not be able to connect them into their personal lives. Often, they will be experiencing great waves of emotion. We all filter the world's energy. In this sea of energy, we are all connected.

Filtering can be done on a more personal level. We may have made a pact with others to help them cope at some difficult time. This could entail being a filter for them. We will filter what they feel and so lessen the impact on them during a hard phase. These pacts are mostly made on a spiritual level.

The telepathic link we share will serve as a connection for the filtering, so we don't need to be physically connected to filter. The emotions, especially fear and anger, can be removed from the one who is being helped. Unfortunately, the one who filters will feel the emotions in their own world. They may experience extreme forms of emotion. Although on a level, they know it is not theirs, it will still have an impact.

Parents, friends and lovers can all filter for each other. We do feel our son's pain or our friend's fear, and filtering for them will ease the whole process. Unfortunately, if we are filtering personal, family and world emotions, our aura can become clogged. Some of these energies can become caught in our energy grid. It is wise to cleanse our aura, and ask Spirit to assist because the bits of energy trapped in our field can create energy flow problems for us.

In addition to working on myself, I like to have others work on me. In that way, I can be sure all the leftover energy snags are removed. While I was engaged in doing much filtering, I felt bigger. My digestion was not good. I was digesting so much on an emotional and mental level that my physical digestion was being affected. We need to be aware of the drawbacks of filtering with a human body because all of that extra energy will sometimes slow it down.

Releasing the energy is the best thing we can do; just letting it go. During the process, we can experience unfamiliar aches and pains. These are not ours. As a filter it is normal to have strange sensations throughout our body. Let the pains go, and remember they belong to someone else.

As a healer we are used as a giant filter to clear and mend the aura. On a world level, we can also experience world emotions and filter them too. It is fine to do this work, but be aware of what is happening in your own body. I did not initially acknowledge the amount of filtering that I was doing. Once I was made aware, I began to operate in a different way. We need to know it is not our emotions. We need to clear our own aura, and to ask others to help us let any residual go.

Choosing to filter

Being able to filter for others and the world can seem like a great gift. I believe it is. However, filtering day and night can take its toll on our own system. Of course, we have our own personal sacred contracts to filter for some people and world events. These were set in place in the Garden of Remembrance. We will honor these promises, regardless of what we wish to do on a human level.

However, be aware that filtering can become a habit. Once we start, we can keep on doing it. Instead of switching the light on and filtering, and then switching it off when it is finished; we can forget. Without realizing it, we may be filtering continuously. This can lead to personal exhaustion, like the little mouse on the treadmill with no time-out.

I also noticed that I was filtering when the person should have been doing their own work. So instinctive was the process, I was engaged without thinking of whether I should be. People will easily transfer their issues onto us, and we can unquestioningly take them on board and filter for them. Not only do we stop their lesson; we also stress our own aura unnecessarily.

Once I understood this, I changed how I approached it all. I asked my gatekeeper to stop any unnecessary filtering. I made a conscious decision to fulfill my sacred contract, but to do no more. I believe that by being a "sensitive" can mean we automatically feel and connect with others. Through this connection, we can unwittingly be filtering for numerous people, which can be draining and tiring for our own energy body.

Sometimes, we can be used to filter when they contact us physically. A hug or a touch can automatically set us up for more unconscious filtering. Be aware of this happening, so you can avoid slipping back into old ways.

When we are on overload our health is weakened, and we can feel exhausted. Processing extra energy places a strain on our own systems. Our digestion, circulation and body functions are under-energized due to the load. If this happens for long periods, then there is too much to process and not enough energy to do it properly. Under the additional load, our own aura can become clogged with the build-up.

It was a happy day when I finally decided to limit my filtering to the promised ones and restrict the others. Consequently, with my intention and the gatekeeper's help, I knew I could begin to feel better, and with less filtering I could vibrate more quickly. This would mean my ability to channel information and healing would be heightened. How good is that?

Automatic filtering

Filtering can take place without our human understanding. Be aware of this truth. Don't be surprised if you automatically filter, even with your intention not to. I discovered that the hospital visit or funeral I knew I had to attend was a filtering excursion. In these situations, I will have a strong urge to be at a particular place. It could be a funeral, a party or a person's home. Even though I may not feel like going, I will know I have to be there. The pull to go is extremely powerful and even if other people try to dissuade me, they can't change my mind.

In the past, I was unaware of these filtering sessions. They happened without me even noticing it. Only recently was I aware of the work being done. On a conscious level, we may not be aware of our filtering until it is finished. Usually, it's only on the soul level we know. Sometimes a close, intuitive friend might open your eyes to the work you have been performing, or you catch on later when it is all over.

Automatic filtering can be extremely tiring. Regularly, I can get a headache and feel totally trashed for around twenty-four hours, and this can often be traced back to a filtering session. If you experience this perhaps you should look back on the last day or week and see what event you were filtering.

Afterwards, I ask for light to refill and cleanse my energy field. I drink more water and try to rest in the following days. Occasionally, I take a salt bath.

Filtering automatically is a gift we have already chosen to give. So be happy, knowing that it helped all those people through a difficult time.

The family and friend "glasses"

In your quest to use your gift, be aware of certain limitations. Being able to get information from the other side can seem simple and easy. Nonetheless, when it comes to those close to us, something can get in the way. That something is you.

Our human and our soul psyche are so intertwined that all guidance passes through our human personality and will carry our personal agenda. If we are emotionally connected to someone and try to read for them, there are many considerations. I have discovered that due to our intimate relationship, our interpretation can become compromised. For example, when my son wanted to know whether he was leaving home or going interstate, I read with my mum "glasses." I wanted him to stay with us. I loved having him physically close after years apart. Therefore, being aware of my prejudice, I gave him my answer with a disclaimer.

Our family and friends know we have the gift, and often they want to access information from us. When you read be fully aware that you could be blocking an answer or letting your personal feelings cloud the message. Normally, if you refuse to read for family and friends, it can create awkwardness. The solution is to explain that you will try to give an answer, but they can't rely on it totally. The "no warranty" clause comes into play here. You can then read for them, but they need to take into account your "glasses."

Another problem can arise. You can get into trouble when your answers aren't what they wish. Generally, your loved ones are used to hearing positive reactions. As parents or friends we encourage and foster their dreams and desires. So when the message does not support their choices or upsets them, you can become the fall guy. This can seriously affect your relationship in a negative way. I have had friends stop ringing me. Some have stepped away for years, only to turn up on my doorstep like nothing has happened. It is the casualty of giving unpopular messages. You have to make a considered judgment. If you think it is important, and you are willing to take the chance, speak. If you sense it could get too messy, keep quiet.

There have been a few times that I have crossed the line. I took the chance, trusting it may alert them to the danger of heading in the wrong direction. Then they could make a more informed decision, from a spiritual point of view. In these cases, I was willing to risk it. Always remember, there is no safety net when we relay unpopular messages. You can be severely punished. Family members and friends can step away for weeks or months. Honestly, people say they want to know. They will beg to be told, and at the time they might even seem open to it all. However, be aware that they can turn on you afterwards.

Shooting the messenger is a common practice. When these people are not in your inner circle, it will not hurt you to the same degree. Still, once they come from your inner circle, it will cut you deeply. Even though you understand what is happening from a spiritual point of view, it will not cushion the hurt. I usually warn the friend a few times before I launch into the reading, but forewarned does not give you immunity. Tread carefully in this area lest you lose a treasured family member or friend.

Asking other readers

As we are all here to help each other don't feel shy about asking other psychics for a second or third opinion. I regularly consult other readers. Just like the filter problem mentioned earlier, even as channels, we can be blind to some issues. Some parts of our lives can be unclear to us, and we can struggle to access the information we need. It is hard to be clear every day. During these times, I normally run it past another channel to receive the validation or extra enlightenment I require.

Readers and healers are real people who have doubts and off days. We might be excellent in some areas, but not as good in others. This is where your network comes into play. This is when two heads are definitely better than one. Working as a team is beneficial for all. It can also stop us from assuming "God status." Even when I know my message was probably right, I will still ask. With important situations, it is wise to get more confirmation.

On other occasions, we may be getting part of the picture, but be missing another important piece. If you tune in you can "know" there is a missing part. You just can't figure out what it is. This has happened to me regularly, and I always ask other people. The fact that we are able to "know" we are not accessing all there is to the situation is a wonderful aspect of spiritual growth. For it shows us how much we have progressed. The fact that we know we don't know is quite a leap on a spiritual level. Never see it as a negative experience.

When I consult another psychic, I give them a general picture of the situation and then let them tune in. By holding back my part, I believe I influence them less.

During conversations with other channels, I have observed that another interesting outcome can occur. Consistently, we may both receive more information as we connect, with one feeding off the other. It can be an amazing experience as more and more comes in from Spirit.

Be open to asking others. Aim to be as clear as possible when it comes to channeling. I believe leaving your ego at the door is a valuable lesson when doing this kind of work.

Strangers as channel messengers

Spirit will also employ another group of people to help you. I call them the strangers. The scenario goes like this. You will be talking to a stranger and during the conversation, you will realize Spirit is using them to give you the answers to questions you may have. Perhaps you have been thinking about taking up dancing again, and while you are with these strangers, they begin to speak to you about dancing classes. Spirit frequently uses these situations to give us the nudge. Many people are open vessels when it comes to Spirit. They can be disbelievers on a human level, but their soul can channel.

Therefore, don't be surprised if the most unlikely ones answer your messages. I have been amazed how frequently this occurs. Whether it comes from your next-door neighbor or the girl at the shop, the message comes directly via Spirit. Once you see this aspect of the work, you will be open to receiving knowledge from the most unexpected places.

These days I ask my guardians to use all means possible to relay the information to me.

Listening to what resonates with you

Regardless of whom the healer or reader is that you choose to see, you need to make sure the messages resonate with you. Everyone is a guide for you. Ultimately though, you have to run the messages through your own being. A good reading should feel right. The messages given should answer your secret questions and give you direction. Any accurate message sits well with you. So if you receive information that does not feel correct, feel free to question it and if necessary discard it.

I stress that all channeled information is merely guidance. Nothing is ever written in concrete. Everything can alter and change as we speak. Many people take everything they are told psychically as the only truth without running it past their own barometer. Some people almost give over total control to the messages. This is your life. God gives us that free will; therefore, listen to your own inner voice.

I find an accurate message resonates with my soul. Occasionally, I experience goose bumps to affirm it in the real world. In short, it feels right. Remember, any message can be lost in translation. Channeling is a tricky business, and mistakes can easily be made. These days, even with my closest psychic friends, I run the messages through my own soul body. In that way, you really will grow personally and spiritually.

If I am unsure, I consult my own guardians and ask to be given clarity. Given time, I often have a knowing, a sense of direction. Our guides are the ones we should listen to first. Learning to tune into your own spiritual guidance will accelerate your growth and strengthen your connection.

Dangling the carrot

There is a particular test Spirit can give you. I call it "dangling the carrot." Free will is always involved, usually your free will. For me, it happens like this. I am presented with a situation, which initially seems good, except that it is not necessarily a forward step along my chosen path. In this case, I know I have total choice. I also know it is probably not what I should be doing as it will be distracting me from my initial purpose.

I have observed that "dangling the carrot" often comes before I am allowed to shift up spiritually. I think it's a test by Spirit to see whether I will stay on track. Perhaps you are starting to do healings and then out of nowhere you are offered a tantalizing job offer. You are tempted as it means money and security. On the other hand, you really feel you should devote yourself to the healing work. Now you have to decide to choose the easy path or the not so easy path.

Over the last decade, I have come to recognize the dangling carrot scene. It comes out of nowhere, and is very tempting. I know it is a test set in place by Spirit. Typically, I am very excited by the new offer. Repeatedly, at the time it happens, I need more money, or I am feeling stuck energetically. It can appear like the perfect solution. These days I never commit to the new offer or proposal without considerable thought. I never give an answer on the spot. I have realized that a pressured answer will not serve me well. I give myself time and think it through. Only after some space and asking my soul for guidance, do I decide.

Of course, when I have to decline my human feels it. Afterwards, I must admit that there is some swearing involved. It can be disappointing to let go of a good deal, especially when times are tough. Nevertheless, following our soul path feels better, although at the time we can't work out how to pay some of the bills.

Remember, the "carrot" lesson is a significant sign of spiritual growth. When you stick to your chosen agreement, you are working at your highest level spiritually.

In these situations, family members and friends can be unhappy about your decision. They may argue or try to put pressure on you. Be aware that they are coming from a human perspective. Try to understand their view and reassure them. However, ultimately, it is important to listen to your inner voice. This is your life, no one else's. Make the decisions that resonate with your inner being.

I find, soon after resisting the dangling carrot, there will be some kind of sign from Spirit confirming it was the correct choice. I have had many dangling carrots and, for the most part, made soul decisions. Be aware that you can make another decision. If you do, another opportunity is generally presented to you. Ask for help and you will be redirected back to the Light.

Issues with faith

Not everything that we wish for will necessarily come true. Doubt can seep into our life, especially when working in the spiritual area, therefore, be prepared to weather these times. Not being privy to the whole plan, it can be easy to lose heart when life does not pan out like we have wished. Perhaps we felt some things would happen a certain way and were disappointed with the outcomes. Maybe some clear reader told us something, and it still has not happened, or it turned out differently. During these times, it can be difficult to keep the faith.

Just remember, it goes with the territory. We live in a world of flux. In my dark moments, I distract myself. I do ordinary activities like visiting friends and immersing myself in movie world. By putting myself in another place, I can keep on the path without focusing on it. Instead of wallowing, I try to keep life as normal as possible. We can feel very angry and disillusioned during these times. Tears of frustration and disappointment are not unusual. I let the tears flow and the anger be expressed because clearing out our human emotions will be better in the long run.

When we are losing faith, doubt can creep into our professional work. Our faith can be tested when the healings and readings are not turning out as expected. It can make us question our sanity, and I know many extremely gifted spiritual workers have had these trying days. During a crisis of faith answers don't always come easily, and it can take weeks or years for some things to unfold. In general, "soon" in spiritual terms can mean next week or five years down the track.

At these low points, I noticed that Spirit may take pity on us and send some sign. This serves to stop us from totally losing the plot. Still, at other times, we will need to ride it out. Unanswered prayers can negatively affect us, as they can sow the seeds of doubt. It's only human to feel like this, so keep calm. To find my way through these difficult times, I ask for guidance and keep moving ahead as much as possible. The most important thing is to keep on the same track and stick to our spiritual intention. If our guardians want us to change course, they will find a way to signal.

As I have progressed through the numerous spiritual stages, these crisis times have surfaced in my life. However, even on my worst days I have always known I was on the right path and never truly alone. In my seemingly loneliest moments, I knew they watched over me. So it will be with you.

On a personal level

Keep in mind that the healing/reading gift is there for you too, so use it daily to help yourself. I believe good channels work on their issues. We can do healings on ourselves and tap into our inner guidance. I suggest we use our own hands to do work on our aura, and regularly use the cards to enlighten us.

It can be hard to be clear when we have an emotional investment. Our own desires can block the truth, or it can be difficult if we want it too badly. As mentioned earlier, I ask for backup guidance if I feel unsure. We can ask for a close friend to be used to convey the same message. In general, there will be signs everywhere to trigger the answer. Songs play on the radio and for the first time we hear the words, or the movie that we watch drums home the same message.

I also ask for confirmation when I am not focusing on an issue. Spirit can then plant the seed. I frequently receive the answer when I first wake up, or when I am engaged in some other activity. We can ask Spirit for messages in the form of words or pictures, or that they use different words to our usual speech, so we know the message is from them. For instance, when I was having a skin blemish checked, I got the word "freckle" and as it turned out the test results showed that there was nothing to worry about.

Everyone finds his or her own connection. Your guides would have already set up a code of connection decided by you. Whether it is with words, pictures, dreams or other psychic friends, you can access the information.

Signs are everywhere for us. Guidance is ever present.

How Energy and Power affect us

It is never a waste to love. The waste is when we choose not to love.

Your "sensitive" aura

The aura is like our personal amplifier helping us to respond to the world and those who inhabit it. Everyone has the capacity to tune in. If we are very sensitive, this can be a good and a bad thing, as we will "pick up" even when we don't realize it. When there are upheavals in the world, many people sense the shifts as these disturbances vibrate in their aura. That is why we are so affected by storms, the tides, the moon and negative events. If more people recognized how tuned in they were into the energy world surrounding them, they would understand their moods and reactions more easily.

In the past, we were connected to our environment, especially when we lived in more rural settings. It is important that we understand that this connection continues to be active in our lives today. As a result, we may find ourselves directly responding to the subtle earth changes. Although I was working constantly with the light, I was initially unaware of my connection to the earth. I knew I used her energy to ground myself because I would feel the energy running through my legs when I did the healing work. Even so, I did not fully comprehend that I was actually feeling the earth energy in my own aura. It came as a surprise to me.

We are always picking up what is happening in the natural world, especially when we begin to work with the light. Sometimes, we may feel swirling in our stomach and dizzy feelings, and later find out there was an earthquake somewhere. Fatigue that comes on suddenly and lasts only for a few hours is typically connected to some earth movement. It is the type of exhaustion that will make us want to lie down for a while, even in the middle of the day.

We are all energy, a small microcosm of the world, so what occurs energetically on a large level will directly affect us. Animals and little children are born with this heightened sensitivity, but we tend to be less aware of it as adults.

In my experience, I have found any spiritual work we do on ourselves clears the aura and subsequently, our sensitivity can be heightened. Be aware of this occurrence when the shifts happen. I believe some of us sense the earth's deeper rumblings, even when the rumblings can't be registered. In a way, our energy body becomes a barometer of the natural world, for we are all interconnected.

When I began to feel the earth changes in my body, I found it daunting, and in the early years I wanted validation of the reason why. These days I accept my aura is sensing a change, and I ride it through. Now and then I get an answer, other times I don't. However, I trust a shift happened somewhere in the world because my aura told me so. Being a sensitive does not mean understanding everything, often it is just accepting the information coming in and not doubting it.

Normally, my friends will have similar reactions at the same time as me. Some will describe it as a weird, unsettling feeling, while others might have strange stomach pains or tiredness. They may feel it in other ways and places to me; however, they are feeling the changes too. After some discussion, they are rather relieved that they are not the only one feeling strange and unbalanced, as there is much comfort when others are experiencing the same outcomes.

It is interesting to note that some individuals who profess to discount these kinds of things will have these feelings, and I believe in some way they too are picking up energetic shifts. We live in a culture where everything has to be proven or tested. Spirit does not work like that. We have to trust. We need to have faith.

Energy vampires

Draining of the aura compromises our health. Some people develop the ability to take energy from others, and these people are draining to be with. We may only be able to visit them for a while. Perhaps we will also keep our phone calls short. Don't feel guilty, it is just self-preservation. I discovered that certain people know how to attach to us and can continue to drain us energetically long after the visit is over.

I had an experience that taught me how much some people can drain from us. After a particular meeting with a friend, I felt very tired. The following morning I woke up with a headache and general lethargy. Then I remembered that the day before when the person had held my hand, Spirit had told me that she was draining me. I was instructed to block the draining, which I did. Unfortunately, it was too late. Being in a social situation, I did it in a quick manner, but the drain was super strong.

Later, I was guided to check my aura with the pendulum and found that all of my chakras were unusually low. Next, Spirit showed me how to remedy the situation. I was instructed to visualize the person standing in front of me. Then I was told to draw back all of my "taken" energy into my aura. I did so. In the following minutes, I repeated the process until I felt all my energy was back. Afterwards, I filled my friend up with light. My headache lifted, and after the rebalancing of energy, my chakras were spinning normally. We can use this process on any person, now, or from the past.

Energy vampires are everywhere. We need to be aware of their existence. They are not bad people, just energy-deficient souls looking for a refill. In our society, we are encouraged to give to others, but giving our own aural energy is unwise. Some people are extremely skilled at sapping others dry. They have probably been doing it forever. Next time it happens to you do not feel concerned, just understand that they have found a way to plug in to your energy field.

I recommend we always protect ourselves. I constantly make it my intention that others will not be able to access me this way. However, be aware that some souls get through the net, and later we may have to do the energy retrieval again.

Yawning

Yawning can be a physical sign for us that we are being drained. I do not refer to yawning when we are simply tired or late at night. I am referring to an unusual type of yawning. Without any reason, while in the company of some people, we may begin to yawn more and more, even though we might have been feeling quite bouncy and energetic before our meeting. It comes on suddenly.

I have found the nonstop yawning can become almost embarrassing. This is a clue that there is an energetic drain from someone. In my life, I have noticed that some of the best drainers are the sweetest people. They don't even know that they are draining us. In a physical sense, we are yawning in an effort to access more energy by drawing it in from the universe. On some level, we detect the drain. After visits like this we can feel exhausted, and it can take time to recharge.

I suggest once you are aware of the drain that you refill yourself with light. Next, cover yourself in a bubble of light. I mentally say, "No one will drain from my aura," and with this intention I block as much drainage as possible. It is not always necessary to know who the person is. Sometimes, I will get it. Other times, I can't work out who it is. All that is needed is protection.

Giving of ourselves is wonderful. However, having the energy drained out of us is not. Don't be blind to those around you. Loved ones can be our greatest source of drainage. For some reason, we don't see them as drainers, and we don't even consider protection. We might think it is mean not to give to those who may have given so much to us.

Then again, sucking energy in this way is never good for anyone. It only replenishes the drainer for a short while, and it would really be better for them to receive healing or learn to access their own energy.

So, next time you begin to yawn incessantly, be aware of what is happening on an energetic level. Refill your aura and put up some protection. A whole you will always be a better you.

White light and the phone

Remember, the phone is a source of energetic connection between people. Although we are not in the same physical space, there is an aural connection between those speaking on the phone. The phone is an unacknowledged place of drainage. I think people don't notice this is happening because they are far apart in the physical world.

However, in the energetic world, we are definitely connected. Before I answer any calls I try to remember to white light myself. Be aware that upset people on the phone can tap in and drain us. I believe that if more people understood this truth, then they would protect themselves energetically.

Once we get into the habit of white lighting ourselves our phone calls will take on a new life. Instead of being a source of drainage, we can be there for the other person and not lose out personally. After the call, I suggest cutting the energetic cord between you and them. If I forget and answer the phone without white lighting, it is easy to white light myself while still on the phone.

Try this process and your phone experiences may be less tiring.

Energy hits

I noticed an interesting aspect to energy connection that I call the "energy hit." It is when others come into our field, get a hit of energy, and then they are gone. Although virtually unacknowledged in our world, it happens every day. When these people make the connection, they are not taking large amounts of energy from us. They access what is needed, and then they are off and away.

When it first occurred, I was bewildered. I would have an unexpected phone call from someone. We would talk for a short time, and then they would be gone. As a rule, I would not hear from them again until the next hit was needed.

These encounters mostly occurred at shops, gatherings and normal activities like sport venues, etc. Now I recognize why these souls are making the connection. They need an energy hit. For these folks, the connection with us is like charging their battery again, a quick plug-in, and then they are happy. Energy hits in themselves do little damage. However, if we are receiving numerous hits on a daily level, we can become depleted. Once in a while is fine, but too many hits can become problematic.

As healers/readers we would have all met these people. They ring us and can't decide whether they will commit to making an appointment or not. I realize that they are after an energy hit and suggest they go away and think about whether they want to come. I rarely encourage the conversation to go on or try to make an appointment with them. If I do schedule a session, they normally cancel or don't show up.

By understanding the energetic hit it helped me to see why these strangers were popping in. It also helped me come to terms with their seemingly, rapid departure. Many came in from the past, and then I never heard from them again. Today, I understand it is the energy hit they are after. Frequently, I send more love and light to help them along their chosen path. Nevertheless, I don't expect anything else to come from the encounter.

After these contacts, we just need to remember to refill our aura, cut the cord connection and send them love and healing.

Reclaiming your energy

Every day we leave our energy around, and over time this can deplete our energy body. Most people are unaware that they leave parts of their aura all over the place. It is in our nature to connect with others and share, but frequently we can deplete ourselves because unwittingly, we leave some of our energy behind.

There is a simple solution. Most nights before I go to sleep, I call my "lost" energy back into my field. I think of my core as a magnet and draw my energy back into myself. It hardly takes more than a thought. The benefits are twofold. Firstly, doing this practice keeps us intact, so to speak, as we continue to maintain a full energy body. In addition, time or space makes no difference. If we choose to we can call back our energy from our first breath here on earth and in that way be fully replenished. The second benefit is that it makes us acknowledge that we are always leaving energy around, and maybe we need to be more aware of this behavior.

There are lots of people out there who want to be given energy, as they can't or won't manifest it for themselves. Some souls do it consciously, while others don't know that they are even doing it. For me, I found the energy vampires were recognizable because in their presence, I began to feel very tired.

Sometimes, we can also be connected to our loved ones so strongly that we inadvertently send our energy their way. If we are pouring out massive amounts of energy toward them, it is like leaving the tap running day and night. It is not good for our aura. Conversely, they are always receiving these bundles of energy from us, whether they want them or not. Worried parents and friends can easily fall into this trap because they can become so involved with the problems of others. Many of us follow this pattern. It is like we feel we have to be doing this all the time as a sign of our commitment.

Nevertheless, we don't need to be working in this way. Once I learnt about this process, I began to look at my own patterns and began to reclaim my energy. In doing so, I also released all the parties concerned.

These days my aura is vibrating a bit differently to others. I sense that instead of appreciating the extra energy, they might find that my energy in their aura is a little irritating. For example, if I am running at one rate, and they are running at another rate, the different vibrations will not always blend well.

It is fine to reclaim our energy. Remember that we are not taking anything from them because this energy is from our aura. With practice, we can draw our energy back and remain whole, which is a good outcome for all. Added to this, we are giving each other energetic space.

I believe that recognizing that energy depletion happens every day will be a valuable lesson in keeping us healthy.

Leaving our energy in other worlds

In past lives, we lived in various parts of this world, and we also had lives in other dimensions. In this earthly dimension, a curious thing can happen. We can literally leave a piece of our soul behind in place and time. This occurs when, on some level in a past life, we don't completely take all of our energy with us.

In this current life, we can do this when we move from one place to another. Without noticing, we can leave some of our energy behind. I think being homesick is a physical sign of this misplacement because a part of us is still back home. It's like we leave, but don't take all of ourselves with us. We all understand this on a human level.

In another situation, we hear people saying how they have to go back to Ireland or wherever before they die. They have an undeniably strong urge to return. On a spiritual level, the reason is that they know a part of them is missing, and in returning, they can collect the lost piece and finally feel complete again. Before dying, some people may have to return to their birthplace to collect the missing pieces. Only then can they leave the earth plane. I think these souls know they won't be coming back to earth for a while. It is like they are completing the circle before they leave.

Another type of energy retrieval can happen. I feel we all have places we dream of revisiting, times in history we are drawn to. Never dismiss this homing device because it is a call from our soul essence. Sometimes, the mere act of returning and reconnecting is enough for the soul to receive completion. I think that whenever possible try to manifest the journey in the physical. If it is necessary, ask for spiritual help with this journey.

However, if you find, for whatever reason, you can't physically return don't be deterred, for all is possible in the spiritual world. On a practical level, you may want to brush up on the places by searching the internet and reading books to activate your soul memory. When I did this work, I imagined myself there in the actual country. Next, I drew back into my aura any energy I had left behind. I asked for any gifts and knowledge I had gained in my stay there to be received. Of course, it would be great to walk through the lush, green fields of Ireland and be able to collect our missing energy, but sometimes, we can't do that.

Frequently, when we are about to move into another area of growth, this missing piece of energy may be crucial. The soul cannot activate the next phase until we retrieve it. Perhaps we were herbalists or palm readers in that life, so by connecting into the energy we can tap into that gift.

Having lost chunks of ourselves lifetimes ago we can drift through many lives without a whole aura. By returning, we have a chance to reconnect to our true self and in doing so, some personal, unresolved issues may finally be dealt with. Collecting our energy from a place will be advantageous on all levels. It is like a healing that we give to our soul.

Soul power

Recently, I was shown how to acknowledge and increase our soul power. Personal power relates to our human aspects, while soul power deals with our soul lives. Apparently, we are able to bring more soul power into our auras purely by our intention to do so. The reason this is very important is because it enables us to connect directly into our soul world.

Many of us come from other ages and dimensions. My life as Wendy Edwards is only one small aspect of my true self. Our soul transcends time and space and within our soul, we hold all the lives and gifts from all of these collective experiences. When we bring more of our soul power into our auras, we become truly who we are.

The way I did this exercise was to focus and "call" my soul power into my aura and simultaneously bring up my power. Over the weeks, I kept doing the same visual and, in doing so, empowered my spiritual self.

As healing channels we use our soul to tap in and connect to the spiritual world. I knew that by drawing in my energy in this way my aura was becoming stronger and stronger. It felt good finally to own all of who I am and could be. To me, it felt like a homecoming.

I feel that this process has other benefits. By drawing in our soul power, we can increase our abilities in other aspects of our life. On a personal level, we benefit as our soul sits more comfortably in our energy body. From a relationship point of view, all our social contacts will be advantaged in this state. We may even have more clarity and insights to offer. Our careers can benefit when we are coming from a soul perspective, and our creative side will bloom with soul power behind it.

As a channel I feel with an increase in our personal soul power, our spiritual gifts can only grow and blossom.

Taking back our energy/power

Giving our power away is not the same as leaving our energy around. Generally, if we have an abundance of energy circulating freely in our aura, we will have strong personal power. Throughout the ages, we have had great leaders who were full of energy and personal power. Jesus, Buddha and Mother Teresa are examples of people with this ability. People would refer to these leaders as charismatic, as they had a special drawing power.

When we are rich in personal power, we have strength energetically. I believe we should never give away this kind of power to others. We can support and help everyone, but when we give away our power, it compromises us.

If we have come from an abusive past, we may have little personal power left. Abuse changes the balance because once we are forced to submit on this level, it is hard to get our power back again. I had lost much of my power long ago. This had meant my aura was more depleted than a normal person, resulting in me possessing less personal power.

Consequently, during my earlier life, I had attracted power-hungry relationships because others could sense my depletion and hook in easily. It was only once I began to work on my issues that I saw the pattern. Inadvertently, I was conditioned to submit to others. Over the years, I have taken back my power, and in the process, strengthened my aura.

I did a visualization to achieve this shift. I remembered the people with whom I had a power struggle. Next, I took back my power, and saw my energy returning and filling my aura. With some very powerful people, I did the exercise five to ten times. Afterwards, I began to feel differently toward them, less affected by them and free at last. Don't think only about the obvious ones. Remember, our friends and family, our boss and others from the past are all possible power relationships for us. Decide to take back the power now. It is a profound exercise with far-reaching outcomes.

Some power relationships began in past lives. Therefore, if we come into this life with an unbalanced relationship with someone, it will continue where it left off last life. All the work we do now will affect this present life. As a bonus, the work we do in this life will alter the next one with that person. It is a win-win outcome for all.

All good relationships rely on an equal balance of power energetically. Balancing the ledger is beneficial for all, as it clears the way for personal and spiritual growth.

Returning power to others

Just like taking back our power is one aspect, there is also the reverse situation. I realized in my life that I had unknowingly taken power from others. It was so obvious, and yet initially I was blind to my part. Once the light bulb went on, I knew the work I had to do. I think we all have to face our own power theft. Over my lifetime, present and past, I must have taken others' power, so I set about sending it back to them.

Once I saw my part in the power plays, I did a visualization. I wanted all the persons involved to receive their personal power back, so I saw it leaving my space and being returned to them. As this was a challenging exercise to do, I asked for help spiritually to make sure it was all done correctly. Afterwards, I refilled my aura with love and light, so I was whole again. In the act of refilling my aura, I was less inclined to try and access anyone else's power.

It takes honesty to face the fact that we have taken away another person's power. We all like to think of ourselves in glowing ways. Unfortunately, this denial will keep us from taking responsibility. Often, it's an unconscious act, a lack of recognition on our part as to what has been occurring.

Sometimes, it must be said that the power takeover was consensual. Perhaps the person needed us to take care of them and run their lives for a time. However, it makes no difference how it goes down. All that really matters is that we send their energy back.

Gradually, I came to terms with my role in the power taking game. I could also see who was enabling me to continue the practice. Do the visual for as long as is necessary. After the first few times, I felt I had sent back most of it. Then in the months ahead, I continued to return any energy I had unconsciously taken. By focusing in this manner, I was certain I was balancing the books, so to speak.

Once we settle our energetic power imbalances, it becomes no longer necessary to lose or receive energy. Our personal power becomes our own.

Giving away our heart energy

Depletion can come directly from any heart connection. People easily give away energy from their heart area, as it is what we have been taught to do. To love is to give, and in our society that can mean giving energy away from our heart chakra. Our society tells us that to give in this way is the sign of true giving. But is it?

Instead of giving love and healing to others, we are taught to give a piece of ourselves, our heart. It is seen as the true sacrifice. This gift is given with no thought of the implications. Our society and religious teachings encourage us to give of ourselves, never questioning the real cost to the human aura.

I believe we are here to give love, while maintaining our own energetic integrity and that by constantly allowing drainage from the heart, we become depleted. Most people are totally unaware of their actions and go on giving from the heart and in the process, becoming weaker energetically.

People in high contact jobs like teachers, nurses, doctors and social workers give to numerous people daily. Unaware of what they are doing, burnout can occur earlier for them than in others. Many times, it comes in the form of breakdowns and illness. If they had understood what they were doing, these dedicated souls could have changed their behaviors and given love and healing, without the same impact on their energy body.

In loving relationships the heart is very important, for it is seen as the source of love. Mothers and fathers give their heart energy to their children, and unfortunately, in some family situations the reverse happens. Some parents take the heart energy from their own children, knowingly and unknowingly.

Another aspect of the action of giving our heart away has to do with wanting to be loved. Often, we give our hearts to those around us in this hope. However, the more we give away, the less we have. When we give a piece of our heart, somehow, our love has a more conditional quality to it. Maybe, we feel on some level that we are owed more because of the gift we have given. Conditional love has a great deal to do with expectations.

Unconditional love comes from a higher level. It flows through us to the other person, with no one giving away the energy from his or her heart. It comes via the heart and travels through it. It is not a piece of the heart. It is a purer love sent with the other person's benefit in mind, and with no strings attached.

When I decided to do my first meditation around the heart energy, it was quite hard. I had a sense of guilt when I took back that energetic piece of my heart. It felt uncomfortable, even though I sent love through my heart to each person. It was extremely difficult to do with my husband and my children, as the old way of giving my heart to others was so ingrained.

We can also do this meditation with those who may no longer exist in our current lives. Although I was estranged from my father, and my mother was dead, it made no difference to the outcomes. Energy is never destroyed, so it was easy to go to each of them and take back the missing pieces. That was a good day! When we have had a complicated history with others, it can be hard to cope. However, once we retrieve our energy it becomes easier. It is the energetic link that keeps us back there. We can do all the mental analyzing and speak until we run out of breath, but the energy tie is where we need to go for this heart healing.

After the meditation, I could feel a shift. By drawing my heart energy back into myself, I could finally be complete again. No matter what the world had in store for me, I was now the best I could be. My ability to move ahead in my own development was advanced, and my ability to be a loving and healing channel was heightened. A whole me could be a better wife, mother, friend and healer.

It was only once I had done the meditation and took back the parts of my heart that I finally felt complete. The more of our heart that we have given away, the more work we may have to do. In a sense, others can have more of us than we have of ourselves.

Giving away our heart energy is not necessary. From this day forwards, give love through the heart chakra. We can tap into a limitless supply of love energy and fill everyone's aura. It is the act of giving, not giving away that we all need to learn. As with all things, when we know better, we do better.

The benefit will be enormous for all, simply, pure love with no conditions. The heart is there to relay love, it is meant as a vehicle to convey energy. With this new approach, our heart chakra energy remains intact and balanced. I believe this information changed my life. We all seek the sense of being whole, without bits missing. In the past, I had never felt whole, but now I do.

Sensing people's energy

I believe we all pick up other people's energy and read it. In our world, energetic reading is how we learn the language of the aura. Without a word, we can gather a large amount of knowledge about a person or a situation. When I speak about energy reading, I am not talking about judging someone else. That is a head process. In society, I believe we often use head processes. I am talking about energy reading which is an intuitive exchange.

Everyone tunes into someone in the first encounter before anyone speaks. At this time, our auras are speaking to each other because in a sense our energy body is hitting their energy body. If we are on the phone or watching them on television, the read can still occur.

Now, some people are very astute readers and some are woeful. Why is that? I think that if our own aura is full of emotional and mental blocks, these will cloud our reading ability. Therefore, the clearer your aura is, the clearer the read will be. Before I did work on myself, my read of people was terrible. It was as if I was half-blind and maybe with such a cluttered aura I was. While everyone else knew the person was bad news, I could not always see it. Of course, at times I was incredibly clear, but then I doubted myself.

Remember, once we are clearer, not everybody sees energetically what we see. In truth, even though we may be outnumbered, it does not mean we are incorrect. In these situations, I know how isolating and unpopular it can feel. For example, we are at work and meet Dick. Now everyone else loves Dick, and there we are screwing up our face and stepping back. There have been times I did not want to feel this way about Dick because it would be easier to be like everyone else. However, when our aura is clear, our instincts are rarely wrong.

Generally, the person in question, in this case Dick, will pick up that we have worked them out, and they can become quite uncomfortable in our presence. In an effort to maintain control, they may resort to playing some games. They might try to single us out from the others. They may try to ridicule us in front of their adoring crowd, or pick an argument. Sometimes, if there is nowhere to retreat, we may have to ride it out. When all fails, they may try to suck up to us. It will feel really fake so try not to gag. These are all power plays.

The gift of knowing can be good and bad. On these occasions, I find saying less is best. We can't help the blind to see, and if we do voice our opinion, we will be met with denial from others. For only once their blocks shift, will they be able to see clearly as well. Remember, we read our world in our own way and time. Always give others the freedom to do the same.

Understanding energy shifts

Our aura changes moment by moment, so when we meet someone we are reading today's aura. Although most auras remain pretty much the same, some people's energy can change dramatically. In my life, I have met people and found their energy to be fine. Nevertheless, in the fullness of time, things have really changed. If we encounter this change in others, we need to understand that our read was true at the time. Keep in mind that all of us have the ability to change our energy daily.

When we first meet someone they can present as a positive energy, and we can't pick up anything wrong. However, a situation can be presented in which they have a choice to do a particular lesson. This can become a vehicle for much personal and spiritual growth. When faced with making a selfless or difficult choice, they may revert to another aspect of their soul. Therefore, instead of making a positive decision they may opt for a more negative one. Negativity in any form always shifts good energy. In my opinion, this energy essentially overrides everything, and thus changes what flows through the chakras. Our aura reflects where we are energetically. So, an aura filled with love and positivity will take on a very different hue to one filled with negativity and ego.

Don't punish yourself thinking you were duped. Of course, there will be times we were blocked from the reality. Nonetheless, people do change their auras due to the choices they decide to make. An angel at the beginning can become a selfish, dark energy given a chance.

In my experience, I have noticed that it can take a while for us to pick up on the shift in the person. At first, there will be small signs. Many times when we are on the journey with someone, we can meet a crossroad where big decisions need to be made. Free will can make us experience growth, or we can merely choose not to deal with the particular issue and go backwards. I have met people who began to deal with their issues and work on themselves, but then decided it was too hard. Unfortunately, when they reached a particular point, it all became too confronting, so they reverted back to where they were.

Initially, I could not figure out why the relationship with them felt so different. I knew I was moving in one direction, I just hadn't worked out they weren't. In some cases, they were going back to the past, back into shutdown mode. It is sad to see someone come so far, and then catapult themselves into darker places, but it is very common. I encounter it in healing work repeatedly. Just as the doorway of their truth opens, they run. I believe they can bury themselves deeper than before and in an effort to stop the real issues from surfacing, they can bolt the doors and become lost.

The outcome all depends on our willingness to grow and deal with our lessons. In my experience, I found that there are few who take up the challenge and follow through. Many begin and when it becomes too challenging, revert to familiar patterns. It's sad, but true. I never give up with these people. If I am no longer on the same path, I send love to them. I ask that they be given other opportunities to face their lessons again, and send them strengthening light for the time when another chance comes up.

We live in an ever-changing world, so why wouldn't our auras change as well? Consequently, I allow myself to change my opinion of others when they change energetically.

See it as a shift in our understanding of how the energies of all can change in a twinkling, and embrace our ability to sense when these changes manifest.

Changing relationships

Our relationships depend on connection, and as we are vibrating beings of light, our basic relationship is energetic. Consequently, when there is a shift energetically we feel it. Frequently, we sense it before there is any physical shift. We know on a deep level that things are about to alter because we can feel the change in our soul.

I have always known when a relationship is on the move. Months before, I get this strange sense of losing the person. Although we are still together, I know that soon one of us will be gone. Initially, I would ignore the signs. Occasionally, I would put it down to my former abandonment issues and co-dependent patterns.

However, in our ever-changing world movement is growth. We have to let others go and find their next challenge. Our society values loyalty and long relationships. These types of bonds are seen as signifying our worth as a friend, as the more friends we have, the higher is our standing in our culture. Furthermore, the longer the relationship, the more we view it as a friendship. In our lives, no one wants to lose a close friend. It hurts and causes us emotional trauma.

In our world, a sign of social success is having lots of friends. Numerous shows on television send the same message. I think there is a very big difference between friends and acquaintances. However, some of us don't learn to see the difference. Once we begin to examine our world and see who the acquaintances are and who are our friends, it becomes easier to understand why there are shifts in our social world. In the past, I had read everyone as my friend. However, many only saw me as an acquaintance. I had not understood how I was being viewed.

There is always sadness and some regret when people move out of our lives, but it brings with it new opportunities and wisdom. These days I know energetically that they are leaving. In some ways, it gives me time to grieve and accept the inevitable. So see this insight as a positive step forward.

They say when the lesson in the relationship is learned it can be over. I believe that with some friendships this can be true. These days I embrace the shift and let it be, and whenever I think of the relationship, I give thanks for having had these people in my life. For each friendship brings us blessings, even if it does not last a lifetime.

Protecting your Spiritual Gifts

In all things be humble, never of ego or power. Become as the smallest atom of the universe in order to be of the Oneness.

Psychic attacks

I have never wanted to be involved in any negative aspect of psychic work. Unfortunately, in the world of the psychic, things aren't so simple. Not everyone uses his or her gifts carefully. Some directly choose to attack, while others may be unaware of their damaging use of the gift. Aural attack is common. I feel it is always generated by our own fears, anger and hurts, and even when unintentional, the attack is propelled by these intense emotions.

The higher spiritual world knows never to harm. The reason attacks happen is because we use our gift incorrectly. If we are upset with someone, we can inadvertently send this energy to them. Often, we may be totally unaware of our ability to do this. When we get cross or upset with someone our auras are intertwined, and without even realizing it, there can be an energetic transfer. Our feelings can be directed to them due to our close connection.

Several years ago I received a healing from a friend of mine. At the time of the healing, I knew she was angry with me. After the healing, I felt really terrible. In giving the healing, she had transferred her negativity. It was probably unintentional, but I immediately recognized it as a psychic attack. To cleanse, I had to release her energy. I did this by washing myself with a cleansing light and cutting the cord to her. Next, I had a salt bath to support the cleanse. The whole experience was a valuable lesson for me.

If we are being psychically attacked it can make us ill. I have found that the attack will manifest within a few hours or days. I have had bad headaches and felt quite sick after one of these attacks. Therefore, if I get ill soon after some issue with another person, I don't discount a psychic attack.

It is unfortunate these attacks occur. Still, I believe with more understanding, we will be aware of this aspect of energy work and know how to deal with it. These days, I will just know it happened. Sometimes, the attacker will be aware of it, but not always.

By being on the receiving end of a psychic attack helped me to understand the power of our thoughts and emotions. This new information made me understand how dangerous it is to work on someone when we have negative feelings towards him or her. To do a healing we tap into our soul energy, and if any negative feelings are hidden there, they will transfer to the person concerned. The transfer can have a very bad effect on their aura.

Therefore, when you are about to do a reading or healing on someone, you need to be very clear about your feelings towards him or her. Your intention might be to heal, yet these emotions could compromise the work. Don't read the cards or do healings when you have this kind of agenda.

There is also another kind of psychic attack. We can be sending negative thoughts or intentions to someone and be aware of doing so. All of us have witnessed someone wanting bad things to happen to another. They may wish them to die or be involved in a car crash. Well, all that negativity reaches the person. Nothing may happen, but the attack has occurred energetically. In these instances, the attacker's emotions may help to manifest a nasty outcome.

Another type of attack uses our psychic skills to disturb someone's aura. There are many advanced beings on earth. Some have been witches and warlocks in previous lives so being able to manipulate energy is familiar territory for them. I know one reader who visited another in a dream, and while the man slept, she threw sand in his eyes. Interestingly, he knew it had happened and confronted her.

I always ask for protection from psychic attack, but it can still occur. On a personal level, I am careful about my feelings towards others. When I am upset, I try to own my feelings, and never project them. When someone annoys me, and I might want to punch them on the nose, I am aware of my part and try to block it from happening psychically. Remember, we are more powerful beings that even we know. Obviously, it is very bad karma to attack anyone, for like a boomerang it will eventually come back to strike you.

Losing your gift

Doing light work is a privilege. It is your pact with your God. The gift is a universal blessing to be used for all. Pure intention should be the basis of all the work that we channel. If we want to channel good light, we have to keep ourselves as a pure channel. I feel there is a great responsibility doing the work.

If we begin to misuse the gift, Spirit can choose not to work through us. I have seen people who fell into bad ways lose their gift. Once accurate and visionary channels, they now struggle to be so. Their readings have become jumbled and inaccurate due to their own actions. I know one lady who began a reading and part way through it, she had to stop. She realized that she was reading herself. If you visit a reader like this, you need to be careful. Initially, you may not be able to pick up the shift in the reader/healer. However, during the session, the information given becomes more and more incorrect, and sometimes you may notice it is underpinned by fear and ego.

Everyone has times when they don't read or heal as clearly. Perhaps they are distracted or too tired, and the focus is not there. However, it is a temporary state and passes. This can happen to the best ones, but when someone loses their gift, they may begin to doubt themselves. Often though, they are the last to know.

Remember, we are only the messengers. If Spirit decides to step away, it will be our fault. They never desert us; it is always we who leave first. Readers and healers are people as well and have their lessons to learn and mountains to climb.

Keep your intentions vibrationally high. We are here to give love, guidance and comfort to others. The gift is not a money machine or an avenue for our ego. It should not be used to exalt us. Keep humble and faithful to those who light the way for you.

Psychic bully

If you have been involved in any spiritual work, you may have met the psychic bully. I describe these people as psychic bullies because of their effect on others. Their victims are normally in awe of the gifts these psychic ones possess, so already the power imbalance is obvious. Unfortunately, whatever these psychics say is taken as gospel.

I divide psychic bullies into two categories. One group wields their power negatively, while the second group is learning how to harness their new gift and may not yet know how to channel carefully. With the second group, their enthusiasm may blind them to times when they are being thoughtless in their delivery.

Often, when we start working with Spirit it is very exciting, and we might want to share our insights with everyone. Yet, not everyone is ready to access the information. At the beginning, we might also be getting loads of information. Initially, I believed I had to relay all I picked up on, so I spoke without regard for the effect of my words. For example, if I thought that someone was going to get sick, I felt that I had to pass on the information.

Now I know better. We will regularly receive insights, but not all need to be passed on. The messages can upset others and bring little comfort. I believe that we need to be careful. For example, if you sense your friend's dad may pass soon, think it through. If he is going, there is probably no way that you can change the outcome. Instead of upsetting your friend, try to use the psychic information in a positive way. Encourage her to spend extra time with him. Support her in her life and be there for the difficult times ahead.

People have free will. They can surprise you. I have felt sure that someone was about to pass, and then the person changed their mind and stayed. If this had happened to my friend's dad, and I had spoken, she would have endured unnecessary suffering. Due to free will, psychic messages can become obsolete. These messages are only valid for the time they are received. If the person makes another choice, the outcome may be different. Furthermore, be aware that there are times people are not in a good place to receive. Ask yourself if the person is ready to hear what you are getting, for a message given on an unsuitable day will not serve its purpose.

Psychics who wield their power negatively might get the messages, but do not consider the feelings of others. Psychic bullies work through the ego. They want to be forceful and controlling, and by being the "oracle" they can take charge of the situation. In the quest to be the "oracle," they blurt out everything they get without any sensitivity towards the recipient. You will recognize them by the effect they have on you. Their messages leave you feeling fearful and worried. Instead of feeling full of hope and comforted, you can feel uneasy, stressed and depressed after an encounter with them.

I had an experience with psychic bullying when I began my journey. I was not very skilled at channeling messages, but my friend was. He could relay much from the other side. In the beginning, it was great. I wanted to know, and he could tell me. However, over the months things started to feel strange. Some of his messages seemed to be coming from his own agenda. It was like his desired outcomes were skewing the messages. It was then that he had stepped into the psychic bully place. Mostly, bullying has a "do as I say or else" quality. We are not given free will. It is their way or the highway, and the predicted outcome of not following their message is dire.

Pure spiritual guidance comes from a higher Source and never scares or threatens you. You will never feel overpowered or frightened, and you will always retain your free will.

I believe psychic bullies work at a lower level, and that ultimately their lust for power and ego corrupts their channeling. Some people I know have been told some dreadful "messages" by certain readers and have been left feeling fearful and upset. If you have visited a reader and felt like this, I suggest you find another channel.

There are often psychic people in our lives. I suggest that if you encounter a psychic bully in your friendship circle, set clear boundaries with them. If they begin a litany of negative messages, shut them down. Be firm and let them know you don't want to hear anything negative. In this way, you protect yourself from their power games. By not encouraging them in these practices, both parties will benefit.

Bullying is emotional abuse. When faced with any psychic bully move away or make boundaries. Keep in mind that true spiritual guidance makes us feel uplifted and comforted. If you have been a bully, even unwittingly, take stock. Aim to work on a higher level and learn to be more discerning. Try to channel in a positive manner and always come from love and light.

Guidance should be given in good light, free of ego and fear.

Harnessing the ego

Everyone has an ego. It keeps us focused on ourselves and is normal and healthy in our society. Unfortunately, in energy work, it can become a stumbling block. I have found that ego can get in our way. Letting go of ego will serve us well because without it, our work can reach higher places, and we can carry more light. Light work is by nature a shared experience. Therefore, there is little room for self-interest.

It is healthy to be proud of our accomplishments. I had to work hundreds of hours to hone my gift. I read continually about all aspects of healing work and practiced at every opportunity. So it is fine to be proud of the effort and time I put into my life's work. Still, I know I don't literally do the work for I am merely the instrument. Okay, I have tried to refine my skills, but ego would have me taking the praise for work done by others. Remember, when we work with Spirit, it is a joint effort.

I feel that ego will slow your advancement spiritually, and bog you down in time. It is good to have a successful reading or healing. You can enjoy the way Spirit can work through us, but as you progress, try to release the need for admiration or praise. I found that doing absent healing and praying for others and the world helped to contain my ego. Silent work is good for the soul. In a world hell-bent on telling us it's all about number one; it is refreshing to work in this way. Push aside ego, and just get on with doing the work. Silence in this case is golden.

Over the last few years, I have tried to become more and more humble. For in the humbleness comes a peace and understanding of our place in the world, and as we become less of ego, our soul can fly.

Personal power

Power can have many layers. While we are working with higher powers to channel, we are also using our own psychic powers to hold the light and relay the information. These powers work synergistically. However, there is also another power to consider. I am referring to our own personal power. Maintaining a strong sense of personal power is necessary when we work in the spiritual realm, as we will be the interface between our human world and the spiritual one. In a sense, we are all God's representatives. Although there will always be guidance, times will arise when you as the channel will be choosing, for we have our own free will, our own personal power.

At the start of my spiritual work, I thought I had to do everything that I was told to do. Now, I understand that it is more empowering when we work together with Spirit and exercise our own free will. In choosing, we stand on our own two feet and own ourselves. For example, people may approach us for work, but we can always choose whom we want to work on and when we want to work. We are not spiritual robots. Our guardians want us to have personal freedom. As I progressed, I came to understand that I did not have to ask permission all the time. Sometimes, I could say no to working on a particular person or at a particular time. As a bonus, I believe that once we step up and become equals that our spiritual work can accelerate even more.

I know I am vibrating more slowly than Spirit. My eyes can't see as clearly or with such an expanse, yet we are working as a team with each member having equal power. It is okay not to work some days. It is okay not to work on some people if we feel unable to. Spirit wants us to pick up our own power. By empowering ourselves, we empower the work, which makes for an excellent work environment.

Remember though, that when it comes to exerting your personal power never treat your fellow spiritual helpers in a disrespectful manner. Some healing channels can become demanding and petulant with Spirit. I have heard them tell Spirit they want this or that and demand that their wishes be fulfilled. When life does not give them what they want, they whine and complain about the universe. These souls think the universe is conspiring against them by holding out and messing up their lives.

Nothing could be further from the truth. We draw to us our lessons. Our life is always of our own making. The universe never operates in the negative way people suggest. I have heard people threaten the universe and state that they won't do some things until they get what they want. Wow, are they pushing it!

Never play power games with Spirit. They will not hurt you, but they will step back and let you figure it out. Generally, we are given several chances to settle down before they stand away and stop trying to guide us. The spiritual world has free will as well. If we carry on like children by demanding and blaming, we can be left to our own devices. Keep in mind that these outbursts can come at a cost. It is normal to feel frustrated and annoyed when life doesn't turn out like we would have hoped, but don't attack the hand that feeds you. Instead, ask for more help and guidance.

We are all special beings so be careful to show respect because abuse has no place in spiritual work. Use your personal power for good and to strengthen the work.

Withholding information

When we do this work others can view us as a powerful source of information; however, we make the final decision to share it or not. There are a couple of times we can choose to withhold information. One choice comes from love, while the other comes from power. When it comes from love, we may withhold the information to protect people. Maybe the message is vague, and we are unsure of the outcome, so we may feel it is in the person's best interest to be quiet. This is to protect the other person from any unnecessary harm.

The other situation is definitely a power play in an effort to hold the upper hand. This is how it can happen. The psychic person alludes to a message concerning you and then plays a cat and mouse game with you. You are left guessing what the message is and as a consequence, feel vulnerable. Occasionally, these games are an attempt on the part of the channel to get us back in line. If there has been a shift in the relationship, these tactics can be used to get your attention so to speak, for whoever holds the information, holds the power. It is a dangerous and nasty game. Messages are meant to give comfort and solace; they are not supposed to be used for personal gain.

People unused to their new gift can step into this area. Control freaks losing control of someone close to them can use this method as well. It is disturbing to be told, "I got something for you, but can't say what it is." It is a sad use of the gift as all it causes is worry and angst. Of course, the purpose is to get us begging for the message, so automatically we are in a diminished position. The messenger holds the power. If we are already in a fragile place, these ploys can unsettle us and make it worse.

My advice is not to play. Refuse to be manipulated and step away. These readers are using power in a very negative and selfish manner. A pure channel will never leave you feeling vulnerable and afraid. I believe these types of power plays come from the messenger's own fear and negativity. In an effort to increase their own sense of power and ego, they use the gift in this manipulative way.

A good reader/healer will never play games like this. They will be aware of your emotional and mental state and channel accordingly. A lower-level reader/healer may not. I have found, for the most part, messages told in this way never manifest and that the outcome will be different. It is almost like their negative approach alters their ability to channel clearly. I noticed that they regularly get the wrong interpretation of the message, and usually they only receive parts of it. Ultimately, their power filter taints the message.

Wielding power in the spiritual world can diminish your gift. Instead of ascending, you can begin to lose all you have gained.

Never use your gift for personal gain. Besides the damage that we can do to others, there will be another cost. Karmically, you will pay, for nothing goes unrecorded in the universe.

The danger for us is getting to love the power we can wield. There is also the danger of becoming a manipulator. Eventually, those who dabble in this way may lose their clarity. Over time, they can't distinguish between their desires and a message from Spirit.

Never use your power in this way as you will eventually lose credibility with those around you.

Be clear when it is you speaking and when it is Spirit. On the days when you can't tell where the information is coming from say so. Use the gift you have been blessed with in truth and with integrity.

Spiritual manners

I have called this section "spiritual manners" because it deals with higher spiritual practices. Just as we have the right to privacy as humans, the same happens in the spiritual world. Therefore, be careful to show respect when using your gift. It is to serve others, not ourselves. This means not prying into other people's lives. Using your gift without permission to tune into others and read them is not on. We would not like someone to rummage through our personal effects, so the same principle applies with spiritual work.

I had not realized this could become such an issue until I experienced it first-hand. At the time, I thought little of it. It was only when I understood how it contravened the laws of Spirit that I began to address it. Helping someone in need brings the gift into play, whereas tuning into everyone's life is different. Do not pry into other's affairs, and don't try to access them energetically. We can send love and healing, but tune in with respect.

Snooping is a direct conscious effort on your part to enter their energetic world without permission. Basically, we are trespassing spiritually. Ego and power are elements in this activity, and being able to do this gives some people a buzz, a sense of power. In my opinion, these people are treading on hallowed ground. All is seen in the eyes of God, yet even God gives us free will and privacy, and so once we embark on this way of using the gift, it becomes detrimental to all concerned.

It is a sign of power playing, like we want to be ahead of the game, the all-knowing oracle. Long-term, it is fraught with danger as relationships can be spoiled. Your gift should never be used in this manner. Of course, there are times we pick up someone may be upset, or we feel we should ring him or her.

It comes to us spontaneously. This is not snooping. These are genuine energetic connections.

I suggest you be aware of this aspect of the work. It is easy to get caught up with being right and becoming the all-knowing psychic, but eventually these practices will not advance your spiritual growth.

Protection from snooping

We can protect our spiritual space if we feel another is invading our field. Frequently, we will be aware of invasion, by the way that we begin to react. In my situation, I develop a guarded feeling with the person concerned. A sense of feeling vulnerable is another sign. Luckily, there is a solution.

To stop spiritual snooping all we have to do is to put up permanent protection on a spiritual level. Usually, we will already be trying to get some distance physically from the person. In a sense, we would have begun to pick up the invasion. As soon as I sense any spiritual snooping, I ask my guardians to block access to the person concerned. With this request, my gatekeeper steps in and blocks them. Immediately, the person I am having snooping issues with is blocked; they are blocked from me and blocked from those close to me.

Even though I want them blocked in this area, I continue to be kind and send them love and healing. In my first snooping experience, it was not something I felt I could easily discuss with the person concerned. In their development and ego place, he would not have understood. Instead, I set up the boundaries with my guardians, and they became the gatekeepers. After a while, the person snooping became frustrated and inadvertently gave me confirmation that the block was working. When next he spoke to me, he complained that I wasn't there energetically for him. In his eyes, I had disappeared. In that moment, I knew the gatekeeper and I had worked together to solve a tricky situation. In my heart, I thanked him for my lesson. I also felt protected and comfortable in my private space.

Be aware, that once you have set up the protection, it will need to be continued. A stubborn person will run around your aura trying to find an entry point. While this is happening, I work with my angels and am vigilant. Eventually, the snoopers tire of not getting access and move on.

No one should cross those personal boundaries without your permission. They definitely should not do so in order to create mischief or wield their psychic power.

Occasionally, they work out what is going on and can become indignant with us. If this happens, be prepared. I noticed the confrontation came in the form of an angry display from them. In my situation, there was a heated argument on the phone telling me off. Picking up this was about to happen, I chose not to argue, but spoke from my heart. Consequently, his anger had nowhere to go. Through it all, you need to remember who is the one crossing the line and stand firm.

Frequently, if these relationships continue, be aware that their messages will not be as good. Without direct access to your energy body, they will be less accurate as they are working on their own interpretations instead of channeling. Potentially, you may be told some incorrect messages, so if you choose to listen be aware of this.

Another worrying outcome needs to be discussed. Without easy access, they could try to punish us with nasty and scary information. We are all human and can be naughty when things don't go our way. Trust your own reactions. If you experience fear in your aura know the messages come from a lower vibration. Some psychics will use the gift to scare us into letting them back in. Don't let them into your energy while they are in this state of mind. No good will come of it.

The fact the person I was blocking knew it was happening was because he was entering without permission. If we want to be upfront we can ask these people why they need to check into everyone's aura. If you think your relationship can handle the truth, tell them you are uncomfortable with the way they are accessing information. Tell them you don't want them barging into your energy field.

Ego and power-driven psychics don't cope well with being shut out. However, every person has equal rights, whether they are using a psychic gift or not. It is your aura, so you decide who enters it.

I found the gatekeeper and I managed to handle a tricky psychic issue successfully. I am sure it will work for you as well.

Being aware of your energetic power

Once we become involved in spiritual work we need to have an awareness of the transfer of certain energy. I have written about this transfer earlier, but want to emphasis it again in this particular section.

We are channeling through our aura to send healing energy to help others. In sending it, we are projecting the energy to them. In a way, it can become easy to forget this, for in projecting energy to another, we alter their energy field. Normally, we never question the projection because, for the most part, we are consciously sending good energy.

Being capable of sending energy means it happens on a daily basis. We think of someone in a loving way, and automatically the energy arrives at his or her energetic doorstep. Thinking negatively will have the same effect.

Most of us are unaware of the energetic power of our own emotions. For example, say we have just had an argument with a friend or family member. After the fight, we may be very angry and be thinking quite negatively toward them. It is very possible for us unknowingly to project and send this negative energy to them. We need to know that we can send energy without meaning to, especially when we are very upset; therefore, being aware of this outcome is extremely useful information. Whenever you are angry with someone deliberately choose to own the feeling and not project it. Of course, all of us have been furious with others and unconsciously sent bad vibes. I suggest you forgive yourself for the past, but make changes in the future.

Being a healing channel holds great responsibility. We are working with the light. Perhaps in other lives we were witches and sorcerers. So, without realizing it, we can activate skills learnt in these less enlightened lives. Having learnt how to manipulate energy can add and detract from this life.

You have free will. Use your gift in goodness and love, and never use it to harm others intentionally. Knowledge is power so use your gift wisely.

Not receiving the healing

There is another game played by some. In an attempt to keep control and prove us wrong they can block the reading/healing. It is a conscious decision to gain power. We may have read clearly, but in an effort to have their own outcomes they will not listen. Usually, these souls have to be the boss at all times, and, in a sense, they can't or won't bow to Spirit.

I have included this outcome in this section because it is a negative aspect of the gift. These people can hound us for spiritual guidance only to question it and reject it. Of course, we all have times when the messages don't please us. However, in this case, the receiver chooses to go the other way deliberately. I had a very good example of this.

I was asked several times by my girlfriend to tell her the truth concerning her impending marriage. I was unsure about how it would affect our relationship and was reticent to channel. Eventually, I did. The guidance was kind, but honest. In the months ahead the person took no notice of the messages. They also stepped away, not contacting me for weeks. Even now the contact is strained and sparse. In another case, one girl has been told by several psychics to leave her husband. Sadly, rather than follow good spiritual advice she remains. It is her fear and also her power struggle with Spirit that keeps her there. In the end, she will have her own way and make everyone's message "wrong." Many who have been told and refuse to listen manifest an illness. Sometimes, they die early in an attempt to escape their miserable lives.

I believe these situations can have negative outcomes, especially for us. Sadly, when others don't receive the information or healing it can impact quite profoundly on us and our relationship with them. It is a disappointing outcome for all.

I have no solution. In their effort to always be right they will try to prove us wrong. I find it really strange because we are not the source for the message or the healing. It always comes from Spirit. There can be ramifications when we choose not to follow the spiritual guidance. The journey is frequently a long and painful one. Bankruptcy and financial problems can occur and there can be much emotional and mental pain.

Spirit is never responsible. We have free will. If we use it to counter spiritual advice, all the blame lies at our feet. I have witnessed people who saw how their parents' lives turned out and vowed they would never be like them. However, given the spiritual choice to change their lives, they chose their parents' path. Simply amazing!

Using your gift can have some negative outcomes. Mostly, they are only due to human choices and power plays. Keep strong in your resolve to help others. Of course, these non-receivers will test your resolve, but never doubt your gift. We are only the channels; the rest is up to them.

Dabbling in dangerous places

In our quest for spiritual knowledge, we can unwittingly be drawn into lower levels. In these areas, we can encounter lost and naughty spirits. I advise against playing around in places with darker energies. Unfortunately, there are those who think it is great to have a household of uninvited spiritual guests. However, they choose not to recognize that the uninvited ones will directly affect their energy.

It is important to keep your spiritual space clear and protected for without boundaries your life can be influenced negatively. I have met people who say they see spirits in their home. Some people have been so freaked out by this occurrence that they need to sleep with the lights on. Surely, if we see these souls and have to keep the light on, they can't be a positive part of our world.

Higher vibrational spirits are full of love and comfort. There is no fear, whereas these lost ones are full of fear and negativity. In our home, they can attach to our aura and energetically affect the environment that we occupy. Some psychics believe these spirits can be attracted to us if we radiate negativity or suffer depression. Others believe we call them in with the signal we put out. It is like the dark parts of us attracting more dark.

Regardless, the only outcome is negative. If you continue to accommodate these spirits, they will eventually begin to infiltrate your real world. Being surrounded by dark energies will mean you may attract similar energies into your human life. I have seen this happen as violent relationships and unbalanced people become more and more a part of these people's daily lives. Unfortunately, those who are coming from light and love will be unable to be in this negative light.

Given time, the good energy friends will fade out of your life, while the ones who thrive in this lower energy will attach and be drawn to you. If you continue to encourage lower entities into your life, your real world can begin to become dangerous. The spiritual world will blur into your everyday life. Unstable humans will gather around, and your own stability may be threatened.

I believe in the law of attraction. Light attracts light. Dark attracts dark. I urge you to take this fact seriously. Don't dabble in these lower worlds. Ask for boundaries to be put up by your gatekeeper, white light your home and ask for protection. Always choose to work on a high level and send the lower energies to the Light. They serve no purpose. All they wish to do is to disrupt and cause fear and doubt.

Certain people have the gift of "seeing" spirits. Our culture puts those who can "see" like this on a pedestal. I believe we need to be discerning when it comes to choosing which energies we allow into our psychic world.

Another aspect we need to accept is the thin line between being psychic and being mentally unstable. Those suffering from mental illness also see spirits. They too are haunted by these visions, so it is very important to keep grounded and to be careful when working in the spiritual realm. Choose who comes into your field. Make firm boundaries because playing around in these areas can have dire consequences. You can go from dabbling around with mischievous spirits to attracting violent people into your life in a very short time. Once alcohol and drugs become involved you are heading for a disaster.

They say that curiosity killed the cat, so be careful in this realm. Of course, if it is where you want to be, do it. You have free will. However, please take note of the danger, and be prepared to ask for protection and help when needed.

Remember that we are like shining lights to the spiritual world; they are attracted like the moths to the light. It is up to us who shares our space, therefore, choose wisely.

Attachments

We can inadvertently attract entities when we are in a dark space. Depression, mental instability and too many drugs can weaken the aura and make us more prone to draw these energies towards us. Many people can walk through their whole lives with these attachments. Dark, lower energies look for the same energies here in the earth plane. Like attracts like. When I see these entities, it seems like they almost hang off the aura from cords, and I have noticed that a person can have more than one hanging from them.

Of course, an energetic leach like this is not going to be good for anyone. You may have met these people. They will exude a darkness, a sense of almost foreboding. I believe many serial killers, and murderers have these energetic parasites. Although it all sounds sinister, it is a common occurrence in the world of energy. For where there is light, there will be dark.

If you feel you have these attachments, you can release them from your aura. The same can be done for others. Like all energy, it can be moved. I see attachments having cords, which allow them to stick onto and feed off the person's aura. The best way to release them is to cut these cords off from the person. Next, I cover the person with white light. I also send the dark ones back to the Light. Before finishing, I ask my angels to prevent them from entering my aura or the person that I am working on.

We have all experienced dark times and possibly attracted these energies. However, most people are totally unaware of this situation. I know I was when I commenced my work. These days, whenever I feel the need, I cut the cords for others hoping their light will remain clear. Naturally, if the person concerned wishes to have these entities with them, it will be their choice. Sometimes, people become so used to their attachments that they can't be without the energy these entities provide. Strangely, to them, the dark energy becomes almost safe and familiar.

We are spiritual beings with the right to choose who crosses into our energy field. Be aware and work to a higher level.

Coming Back to Earth

Wish goodness for all people. For how great is their soul and what lessons they have set in place few men know.

Coming back too early

Once we cross over to the other side, we begin to work on the life we have had on earth. Our spiritual helpers give much healing, and we are able to see clearly the areas needing attention. There is time given to heal and rest, and we are encouraged to stay in this place until we complete our spiritual lessons. Hence, when we move to the next life becomes our choice.

Unfortunately, some souls choose to come back too early. Like those patients who discharge themselves from the hospital before they should, these souls return to earth too soon. Sadly, without the necessary debrief and healing time, they can come in unprepared. Returning early makes us vulnerable on all levels. Still damaged from the last life, we can begin on an uneven platform. In addition, by skipping the review time, our issues and lessons remain unresolved. If we come back earlier it is actually harder for us. On the other side, the energy is lighter and more loving, and working there on our issues is so much easier. In the healing rooms, there is also more help available.

In my opinion, you can recognize early entry by early exit. Early entries are more likely to suicide or get heavily involved in addictive behaviors. Due to incomplete healing and time spent on the other side, they come in with less ability to function well. When the soul is contemplating an early return to earth, there will be a discussion with their spiritual guardians. For the most part, they will be advised to remain in the spiritual world and receive healing because coming back too soon makes us so vulnerable. In spite of this, some souls won't listen, and start the process of re-entering the earth's sphere. Some miscarriages are a result of the soul deciding to go back and not to be born again at this time. Sometimes, young babies who pass over early have made the same decision. Once here, they decide it is too hard, change their mind and go back. Not all deaths are lessons for those on earth; some are return trips.

It is human nature to avoid pain, but coming back without adequate healing will prove to make life very challenging. As a healer/reader these souls may be drawn to you. Spirit will guide you when you work on them, thus enabling the person to receive the healing on earth. Healers are sometimes their only saving grace; indeed, it is generally only spiritual healing that will help them bridge the gap. Healing can be given to help them to remain on earth and move ahead. Channeled messages can assist them in beginning to deal with the issues that should have been faced. Their helpers from the other side will be able to work through us and assist in their progress.

Coming back too early is a common occurrence. In our haste to avoid soul learning we can try to escape. Nevertheless, it will have to be dealt with in the fullness of time.

Connections to the other side

There are situations when we can't easily connect with deceased ones. Soon after crossing many souls are involved in life review and extra healing. During the crossing, much energy is used, and you could say some are "jet-lagged." As a rule, many families want to contact loved ones, but can't feel them around. I think there are a couple of explanations.

Essentially, we may be so full of grief and emotion that Spirit can't get through into our aura because there is too much clouding us. When the aura is choked with sadness and tears, it becomes like a fog. Our emotions can completely cover us, so that nothing else gets in. It is like being in grey cotton wool. Even if our loved ones wished to reach us, they would find it difficult. Fortunately, in time the fog begins to lift, and communication can commence.

Another reason concerns the person who has passed. Frequently, they are being rested. Having crossed, they review their lives and commence any necessary healing. While in the healing rooms, they can be impossible for us to reach psychically. In effect, they are busy and even a clear channel can have difficulty accessing them. In a few cases, their healing might have commenced on the human side. Issues and problems might have been addressed, and the healing started, and if they had been given spiritual healing on earth they may have already made the necessary shifts. In these situations, they can be accessed earlier than usual.

However, in the majority of cases, they would have just begun the real work once they crossed. If there has been much left undone the person can be in the healing rooms for ages, and while there, access can be denied. For example, after addiction rehab is needed until the soul is better. As with all things, this process can be lengthy, especially if the soul is stubborn and uncooperative.

Don't feel bad if you can't "feel" your deceased loved one, and don't blame the channel if your dad or friend doesn't come through. It is a complex system. In my experience, certain souls won't come in strongly even decades after passing. Unfortunately, not everyone wants to say sorry or send love. Remember, just because we cross does not mean our soul personality changes. We are always given opportunity, but stubborn souls live in all dimensions. Your difficult mum has not necessarily become a different person once she passed into the next dimension. She will choose whether she makes the changes. It is not a given.

There are various planes once we cross, and the access is not always simple. If the soul is in a particular vibrational plane, they may find it hard to connect to our earth. The vibration that they have chosen to work in may make connection more challenging. If we are meant to connect it will happen.

If you can't connect, continue to send your love and prayers. It is like the answering machine. When the time is right, they will get back to you. Trust in universal goodness and have faith.

Crossing and coming back

It is a normal occurrence to cross and come back. It has been happening forever. The crossing often signals a transition for the person involved. I crossed and returned. I saw the river and my mum (deceased) on the other side of the river, and next to her stood a tall figure radiating brilliant, white light. My mum spoke to me without using her mouth. It was telepathic communication. Then I was back on earth. The following years were filled with personal revelation and finally dealing with my childhood.

I have heard many crossings are similar. I believe the crossing becomes a time to remind us about the sacred vow we made before we were born. It is an opportunity for us to return to earth and get back on track. It is easy to block the truth and lose our way. There are so many distractions. Nevertheless, once we have crossed there is nowhere to hide, and there are no more excuses. It is like we know the time is up, and we need to decide.

Most of the returnees have enormous life changes. Their work completely alters. Some relationships end, while new ones commence. There is a great amount of sorting that occurs after a near-death experience. In my case, my life was turned upside down.

There is another reason we cross and return. In particular cases, some cross only to be told it is not their time, and they are sent back. If we are not supposed to die, we will be returned to serve out our days. People can lose their will to live here and choose to let go. Some might try to go back too early. In these situations, Spirit will assist them in returning. There is no penalty. Depressed souls can want to go home so badly that they lose the will to live and do foolish things. Although it might only be a phase they are going through, they can decide to commit suicide. In spiritual terms, many unsuccessful suicides are mostly successful returns.

We can also get accidentally caught up in a situation and cross unintentionally. Mistakes happen. If you get sent home, and it is not your time, you will be returned to earth. On our side, it will appear as a miraculous recovery. These are the people who survive against the odds and pull through when all hope is gone. In reality, the miraculous recovery was totally orchestrated by Spirit, for all can be "fixed" in spiritual terms.

Trust in the wisdom of the universe. The humans who "die" and return bring with them hope for others of the existence of the other side. Meeting another person who has crossed and come back to tell the tale brings hope and light. I believe when we cross, we bring back the Light. That is part of the returning.

If you have crossed and returned, I hope you have found your peace. If you have never crossed don't be envious, for we all cross in time.

In conclusion

Each act of kindness is noted in the spiritual realm and seen as a glistening jewel.

As a channel you must now decide how your path will be. I hope you have gained some wisdom from this book, and it helps in your healing journey. As always, we must ultimately write our own book, the book of our truths. For me, the path has been quite wondrous and exciting. The more I learn, the less I feel I know. Perhaps that is the beauty of the spiritual work as it unfolds and changes day by day.

This book was written specifically for those of us wanting to be more actively involved in working with the Light. I know you will take the answers and information that you need to help you along the way. I also know that at different times you may return to reread this book when you need to.

For me, it has been a great learning and an exhilarating experience to share all that I have been taught by Spirit and other wise channels. Ultimately, none of the wisdom belongs solely to us, as it resides for all in the Oneness.

I send blessings to you on your chosen path and wish for your way to be lined with love, light and the abundance of the universe. Be joyful in your learning and loving in your soul.

With love,
Wendy x

After an electrical accident, Wendy Edwards' life changed from teacher to healer. While living in Australia, she has worked on hundreds of people using her newly found healing and channeling gift. As part of her sacred contract, she was guided to write these books and share the wisdom from above.